Holiday
SNACKS&
APPETIZERS
AND OTHER CHRISTMAS FUN

Contents

Introduction

According to a popular song from the 1960s, Christmas is "the most wonderful time of the year." And why not? The season is filled with delicious foods, heartfelt gifts, and beautifully decorated trees. Better yet, behind all of the fun lie the peace and goodwill of a miraculous Baby, born in Bethlehem so many years ago.

This book celebrates all of that: the cookies and candies, the cards and presents, the wreaths and ornaments—as well as the birth of the Savior. Recipes, gift ideas, stories, and Scriptures fill the pages of this remarkable volume, which comes with two compact discs of melodious Christmas songs.

Pop in a CD and page through *Holiday Snacks & Appetizers and Other Christmas Fun.* In the first section, you'll find nearly one hundred pages of tasty snacks and appetizers—including beverages, dips, and cookies. Next, an entire section on Christmas sweets offers even more dessert recipes, including cakes, candies, and no-bake treats. Third, a marvelous collection of gift ideas will help you please everyone on your list with homemade presents and creative wrapping ideas. And finally, for decorating home, office, or church, there's a section of 101 tree-trimming ideas.

Christmas truly is the most wonderful time of the year. Make this year's celebration even more memorable with *Holiday Snacks & Appetizers and Other Christmas Fun.*

Holiday
SNACKS & APPETIZERS

"Today in the town of David
a Savior has been born to you;
he is Christ the Lord.
This will be a sign to you:
You will find a baby
wrapped in cloths
and lying in a manger."

LUKE 2:11–12

Christmas is a tremendous time of joy,
and there is no better way to celebrate than to
share this time with friends and loved ones.
Our Lord calls us to fellowship together,
so let us do that by sharing our homes
and our friendship, and add to the fun
with some good food to share.
May the joy of the Christmas season be with you
this holiday and at all times.

*"He has shown kindness by giving you
rain from heaven and crops in their seasons;
he provides you with plenty of food
and fills your hearts with joy."*

ACTS 14:17

Appetizers

*My soul will be satisfied
as with the richest of foods;
with singing lips my mouth will praise you.*

PSALM 63:5

Sweet and Sour Pork Appetizers

1 lb ground cooked ham
1 lb ground pork
2 c bread crumbs

1 c milk
2 eggs, beaten
1 tsp salt

Mix and shape into meatballs.

SAUCE:

1½ c brown sugar
¾ c vinegar

¾ c water
1 tsp dry mustard

Pour sauce over meatballs and bake uncovered at 325° for 40 minutes.

Sour-Sweet Wiener Tidbits

1 c currant jelly
1 lb wieners or cocktail sausages

¾ c prepared mustard

Combine mustard and jelly in top of double boiler; heat. Add bite-sized wieners; heat thoroughly.

Mini Meat Pies

Tart shells, baked

FILLING:

1 lb ground veal or beef
1 lb ground pork
1 can cream of mushroom soup

1 medium onion, chopped
Salt, pepper, garlic to taste
Butter

Sauté onions in butter, add meat, and cook until meat loses color. Add spices and soup. Cool filling before using.

Microwave Mozza-Mushrooms

4 slices bacon, cooked and crumbled
12 medium fresh mushroom caps

12 cubes of mozzarella cheese
Grated Parmesan cheese

Place equal amounts of crumbled bacon into each cap. Top with cheese cube. Place on microwave tray or glass dish. Microwave on high for about a minute or until cheese melts. Sprinkle with Parmesan cheese and serve.

Honey-Glazed Chicken Wings

3 lb chicken wings
$\frac{1}{3}$ c soy sauce
2 tbsp oil
2 tbsp chili sauce (or ketchup
   or barbecue sauce)
$\frac{1}{4}$ c honey

1 tsp salt
$\frac{1}{2}$ tsp ground ginger
$\frac{1}{4}$ tsp garlic powder (or
   1 clove garlic, minced)
$\frac{1}{4}$ tsp cayenne pepper

Separate wings at joints. Mix remaining ingredients. Pour on chicken.
Cover and refrigerate, turning chicken occasionally, at least one hour
or overnight.

    Heat oven to 375°. Drain chicken, reserving marinade. Place
chicken on rack in foil-lined broiler pan. Bake 30 minutes. Brush
chicken with reserved marinade. Turn chicken and bake for another
30 minutes or until tender.

Herb and Cheese-Filled Cherry Tomatoes

1 (4-oz) pkg cream cheese, softened
½ tsp dried dill weed

1 tsp milk
15–16 cherry tomatoes

Combine cream cheese, dill, and milk until blended. Remove top and seeds from tomatoes. Drain tomatoes upside down on paper towel for a few minutes. Fill with cream cheese mixture. Chill or serve immediately.

Pita Bites

1 bag pitas, halved and cut into triangles, or minisized pitas
1 c mayonnaise
1 onion, chopped

½ c slivered almonds
½ lb cheddar cheese
6 slices crumbled cooked bacon

Combine everything except pitas. Spread mixture on top of pitas. Bake at 400° for 8–10 minutes.

Guacamole Bites

2 cans refrigerated crescent
   dinner rolls
$\frac{1}{2}$ tsp cumin
$\frac{1}{2}$ tsp chili powder
1 container ($1\frac{1}{2}$ c) guacamole
   or 3 ripe mashed avocados

1 (8-oz) pkg cream
   cheese
1 tomato, chopped
$\frac{1}{4}$ c bacon bits
$\frac{1}{4}$ c sliced ripe olives

Separate crescent rolls into long rectangles, place on un-greased cookie sheet, and press over bottom of pan. Sprinkle with cumin and chili, bake for 17 minutes at 375° or until golden brown. Cool.

Combine guacamole and cream cheese until smooth, spread over crust, and chill. Top with remaining ingredients.

Makes 60.

Cheesy Mushroom Rounds

2 (8-oz) tubes refrigerated
   crescent rolls
2 (8-oz) pkg cream cheese,
   softened
3 (4-oz) cans mushroom
   stems and pieces, drained
   and chopped

1¼ tsp garlic powder
½ tsp Cajun seasoning
1 egg
1 tbsp water
2 tbsp grated Parmesan
   cheese

Unroll crescent dough into 2 long rectangles; seal seams and perforations.

Combine cream cheese, mushrooms, garlic powder, and Cajun seasoning. Spread over dough to within 1 inch of edges. Roll jelly-roll style and seal edges and place seam-side down on a greased baking sheet.

Beat egg and water, brush over roll, and sprinkle with cheese.

Bake at 375° for 20–25 minutes or until golden brown. Cut into slices. Makes 16.

Mushroom Nappies

(can be made ahead and frozen)

3 tbsp butter or hard margarine
1 c onion, chopped
2 c fresh mushrooms, chopped
1 c grated mozzarella cheese
1/4 c grated Parmesan cheese
1 tsp parsley flakes
1 large egg

1/2 tsp whole oregano
Salt
12 slices white bread
1/3 c butter or hard
   margarine, softened
3 yellow cheese slices

Beat egg, chop butter into chunks with a fork and add to egg, then stir in onion, mushrooms, cheeses, parsley, oregano, and salt. Set aside.

Cut off crusts from bread slices. Roll each slice lightly with rolling pin to flatten. Butter slices. Cut each slice into 4 squares. Press, buttered side up, into tiny muffin tins. Fill with mushroom mixture using about 1 1/2 teaspoons for each one.

Cut each cheese slice into 16 small squares. Put 1 square on top of each tart. Bake in 350° oven for 20–25 minutes. Makes 4 dozen.

Crab Wonton

(freezes well)

3 tbsp cornstarch
1 (8-oz) pkg cream cheese, softened
1 (8-oz) can crabmeat, drained
½ tsp Accent seasoning

2 tbsp green onion, minced, including some tops
1 (1-lb) pkg wonton wrappers (about 60)

Lightly dust waxed paper with cornstarch and set aside. Cream cream cheese; blend in crab, Accent, and onions. Place ¾ teaspoon in center of each wonton piece. Moisten the edges with water then fold into a triangle. Press edges to seal. Fry a few at a time in vegetable oil at 365° until golden. Turn once. Drain; serve. Makes 5 dozen.

Crab-Stuffed Mushrooms

1 lb mushrooms
1 (6-oz) tin crabmeat
1 egg, well beaten
$\frac{1}{4}$ c fine bread crumbs
$\frac{1}{4}$ c tomato juice
1 tsp lemon juice
Dash Tabasco

1 tsp onion, finely
    chopped
2 tsp celery, finely
    chopped
$\frac{1}{2}$ tsp salt
$\frac{1}{2}$ c bread crumbs
$\frac{1}{4}$ c melted butter or
    margarine

Mix first 9 ingredients and fill mushroom caps. Toss remaining bread crumbs with melted butter and sprinkle over filled caps. Brown 6 inches from heat 5–8 minutes, or bake in 350° oven 15–20 minutes.

Tiny Ham-Stuffed Tomatoes

1 pt cherry tomatoes
1 (4$\frac{1}{2}$-oz) can deviled ham

2 tbsp sour cream
2 tbsp horseradish

Thinly slice tops from tomatoes. Remove pulp and drain shells upside down on paper towels. In small bowl combine remaining ingredients; fill tomatoes and refrigerate. Makes approximately 20.

Sausage-Cheese Balls

1½ c all-purpose
   baking/biscuit mix
16 oz or 4 c shredded sharp
   cheddar cheese

2 lb ground pork sausage
½ c finely onion, chopped
½ c celery, finely chopped
½ tsp garlic powder

Mix all ingredients and roll into 1-inch balls. Bake 15 minutes on ungreased cookie sheet at 375°, until golden brown. Makes about 6 dozen.

Cheese Puffs

¾ c margarine or butter
1 (3-oz) pkg cream cheese
8 oz sharp cheddar cheese
Tabasco sauce
Garlic salt
Worcestershire sauce

2 egg whites beaten
   stiffly
1 white sandwich
   loaf of bread
   (frozen)

Melt butter or margarine and cheeses together. Add seasoning. Fold in beaten egg whites.

Cut crusts off frozen loaf. Cut bread in cubes and dip each cube in cheese mixture. Place on greased cookie sheet and set in fridge overnight. Bake at 350° for 15 minutes.

Honey-Soy Chicken Wings or Ribs

$\frac{1}{2}$ c honey
$\frac{1}{4}$ c soy sauce
1 clove garlic, crushed

1 tbsp ketchup
Seasoning salt, to taste

Mix and marinate ribs or chicken for at least 2 hours. Bake at 350°
for 45 minutes on foil-lined baking sheet, turning once.

Chinese Chicken

1 can crushed pineapple
$\frac{1}{2}$ c water
$\frac{1}{2}$ c vinegar

$\frac{1}{2}$ c brown sugar
Cornstarch

Mix and thicken with cornstarch. Baste chicken wings or drumettes
for 2 hours. Bake at 350° for 45 minutes on foil-lined baking sheet,
turning once.

Cocktail Meatballs

1 lb ground beef
1 egg
½ c bread crumbs
½ c ketchup

1 tbsp parsley flakes
½ tsp onion powder
½ tsp seasoned salt
Pinch pepper

SAUCE:

1 (14-oz) bottle hot or
   regular ketchup

1 (12-oz) jar apple jelly
1 (12-oz) jar currant jelly
2 tbsp cornstarch

In a bowl combine meatball ingredients. Mix well and shape into 1-inch balls. Place on a rack in a shallow pan. Bake at 350° for 10–15 minutes. Combine ketchup and cornstarch. Stir in jellies. Place on top of meatballs.

Magic Meatball Sauce

1 (1-lb 10-oz) jar of Ragu, traditional recipe
1 (18-oz) bottle Kraft Spicy Honey BBQ sauce
1 can cream of chicken soup

Melt can of soup over low fire or in microwave. It is almost solid and will cause your sauce to be lumpy if you don't melt it first. Add all ingredients into Crock-Pot and add cooked, defrosted meatballs. Simmer until ready to eat.

Toasties

1¼ lb lean ground beef
½ c grated cheese
½ c green pepper, chopped
1 can mushrooms, drained
1 can cream of mushroom soup
¾ c bread crumbs
½ c onion, chopped

1 egg
Dash of
    Worcestershire
    sauce
Salt and pepper
Slices of bread
Butter

Mix well all except for last 2 ingredients. Using a cup or round cookie cutter, slice bread into rounds. Butter one side of rounds and put buttered side down in muffin tins. Add mixture and bake at 375° for approximately 25 minutes. Makes 42 toasties.

Bologna Bites

Place a piece of bologna on top of a microwave-safe cup. Microwave 30 seconds. Let cool.

When you flip it up, you have a little container. Stuff with grated cheese, beans, eggs, veggies, croutons, and a creamy dip, etc. Use your imagination!

No-Crust Quiche

2 c grated cheese (cheddar or
    Swiss)
1 onion, coarsely chopped
2 (10-oz) cans sliced
    mushrooms (drained)

2 tbsp butter
16 Ritz crackers
8 eggs
Salt and pepper to taste

Sauté onion and mushrooms in butter. Crush crackers. Add remaining ingredients, except mushrooms and onions which are added at the end. Fill muffin tins ½ full or use two 9-inch pie plates and bake at 325° for 35 minutes.

OPTIONS:
You can add 8–10 slices bacon, fried and crushed, or shrimp pieces.

Cheddar-Bacon Truffles

6 slices side bacon, chopped
8 oz old cheddar cheese, cubed
$\frac{1}{4}$ c butter, cubed
2 tbsp each parsley and green
  onions, chopped

2 tbsp drained hot banana
  pepper rings, or to
  taste
$\frac{3}{4}$ c toasted pecans, finely
  chopped

Cook bacon until crisp; drain well, reserving 1 tablespoon drippings, and set aside. Combine cheese, butter, parsley, green onions, and banana pepper rings and blend in food processor. Add bacon and drippings and process until bacon is finely chopped. Chill mixture 3 hours or until firm enough to roll into 2 dozen balls, 1 inch in diameter. If mixture softens during rolling, return to refrigerator. Roll balls in chopped pecans and store in refrigerator up to 2 days before serving. Serve with crackers.

Hot Mushroom Turnovers

1 (8-oz) pkg cream cheese,
   softened
All-purpose flour
Butter or margarine, softened
$\frac{1}{2}$ lb mushrooms, minced

1 large onion,
   minced
$\frac{1}{4}$ c sour cream
1 tsp salt
$\frac{1}{4}$ tsp thyme leaves
1 egg, beaten

About 2 hours before serving, in a large bowl beat cream cheese, add $1\frac{1}{2}$ cups flour, and $\frac{1}{2}$ cup butter, and mix until smooth. Shape into ball, wrap, and refrigerate 1 hour.

In 10-inch skillet over medium heat, place 3 table-spoons butter, and cook mushrooms and onion until tender, stirring occasionally. Stir in sour cream, salt, thyme, and 2 tablespoons flour; set aside.

On floured surface with floured rolling pin, roll half of dough $\frac{1}{8}$-inch thick. With floured $2\frac{3}{4}$-inch round cookie cutter, cut out as many circles as possible. Repeat.

Preheat oven to 450°. On one half of each dough circle, place a teaspoon of mushroom mixture. Brush edges of circles with some egg; fold dough over filling. With fork, firmly press edges together to seal then prick tops. Place turnovers on ungreased cookie sheet and brush with remaining egg. Bake 12–14 minutes until golden. Makes about $3\frac{1}{2}$ dozen.

Hot Crab Triangles

1 (8-oz) pkg cream cheese,
   softened
½ tsp dry mustard
1 tbsp milk
Dash cayenne
1 (6-oz) can white crabmeat,
   drained

2 tbsp minced chives or
   green onion
2 tbsp blanched almonds,
   finely chopped
12 slices firm-type white
   bread, crusts trimmed
Paprika

Beat cream cheese, mustard, and milk until fluffy. Add cayenne, crab, onion or chives and mix well. Add almonds and mix again. Spread generously on bread slices. Sprinkle lightly with paprika. Cut each slice into 4 triangles and place on baking sheet. Bake at 400° 10–12 minutes, or until well browned. Serve on cocktail picks. Makes 4 dozen.

Teriyaki Meatballs

2 eggs
2 lb ground round steak
½ c cornflake crumbs
½ c milk

2 tbsp grated onion
1 tsp salt
¼ tsp pepper

Mix and form into meatballs, about 1½ inches in diameter, and bake 45 minutes at 300°, turning and braising every 15 minutes.

SAUCE:

1 c soy sauce
2 tsp ginger juice or 1 tsp
   powdered ginger

½ c water
2 cloves garlic,
   minced
1 tsp sugar

Combine and place over meatballs, cooking until heated through.

Stuffed Bacon Rolls

¼ c milk
1 egg, beaten
2 c soft bread crumbs,
    about 3 slices
10 or 11 slices bacon

1 c Granny Smith apple,
    finely chopped
1 tbsp onion, finely
    chopped
1 tbsp parsley, snipped
Salt and pepper to taste

In a mixing bowl, combine milk and egg. Add crumbs, apple, onion, parsley, salt, and pepper; mix well.

Cut each slice of bacon in half crosswise. Shape crumb mixture into balls, using one rounded tablespoon for each. Wrap each ball in half bacon slice; secure with a wooden pick. Place on a wire rack set in a 15x10x1-inch baking pan. Bake at 375° for 30 minutes or until bacon is brown. Makes 20–22.

Shrimp-Bacon Bites

1 c cleaned cooked shrimp, or 1 can
½ clove garlic, slivered

½ c chili sauce
8 to 10 slices bacon

Mix shrimp and garlic; pour chili sauce over mixture. Cover and refrigerate, stirring occasionally for several hours.

Cut bacon slices into halves. Fry bacon until partially cooked; drain. Wrap each shrimp in bacon piece and secure with wooden pick. Broil 2–3 inches from heat until bacon is crisp. Makes 16–20.

Mushroom Treats

Fresh bread
3 tbsp onions, finely chopped
$\frac{1}{4}$ c butter
$\frac{1}{2}$ lb mushrooms, finely chopped
2 tbsp flour
1 c heavy cream
$\frac{1}{2}$ tsp salt
$\frac{1}{8}$ tsp cayenne
1 tbsp parsley
1 tbsp chives
$\frac{1}{2}$ tsp lemon juice
Parmesan cheese

Using a cup, cut bread into circles the size of a muffin tin. Press bread lightly into bottoms of muffin tins and bake 10 minutes at 400°.

Sauté onions in butter. Add mushrooms and cook on low heat 10–15 minutes. Remove from heat and add flour and cream; bring to a boil and simmer 1–2 minutes. Add spices and lemon juice, and let cool.

Fill cups with mixture; put a dot of butter on top and sprinkle with Parmesan cheese. Bake at 350° for 10 minutes (broil for 1 minute if needed). Makes 4 dozen.

Pasta Rolls

FILLING:

1 (8-oz) pkg plain cream cheese, softened

4 oz sharp cheddar cheese, shredded

Dash cayenne pepper

½ c chopped unsalted cashews, lightly toasted

2 tbsp parsley, finely chopped

Combine cheeses and cayenne and beat until smooth. Stir in nuts and parsley.

ROLLS:

Remove crusts from slices of fresh bread. Roll with rolling pin to flatten and thin. Butter the bread slightly and spread filling to the edges. Roll up jelly-roll fashion or make small sandwich fingers or squares. To store, wrap well in plastic wrap and freeze no longer than 2 weeks.

Cheese Pitas

½ pt cottage cheese
4 oz ricotta cheese
1 oz feta cheese
1 egg
½ green onion, chopped

1 tbsp minced
  parsley
6 sheets filo dough
2 tbsp melted butter

Beat together cheeses, egg, onion, and parsley. Lay out the filo dough and cover with plastic wrap. Using one sheet at a time, brush lightly with butter. Cut each sheet into 6 strips about 3 inches wide. Place a teaspoon of filling at one end of each strip. Fold like a flag (folding/rolling in triangles to capture filling in middle, layering filo around it).

Place seam down on greased baking sheet. Brush tops with melted butter. Bake at 350° for 15 minutes or until golden brown. Makes approximately 3 dozen.

Swiss Cheese and Ham Tartlets

2 c finely shredded
   Swiss cheese
$^2/_3$ c cooked ham, finely
   chopped
$^1/_3$ c green onion, chopped

$^1/_3$ c sour cream
24 frozen unbaked
   3-inch tart shells
Salt and pepper to
   taste

Combine cheese, ham, onions, and sour cream and mix well. Add salt and pepper. Place tart shells on large baking sheet. Bake at 375° for 10 minutes only. Remove from oven and divide cheese mixture evenly among shells. Return to oven and bake 10 minutes more or until filling is hot and melted.

Coconut Shrimp

SHRIMP:

1 pouch shaker chicken
    coating mix
1 c coconut, toasted
$^1/_2$ tsp curry powder

$^1/_4$ tsp cayenne pepper
1 lb shrimp, fresh or
    frozen, thawed
1 egg, beaten

Combine dry ingredients. Dip shrimp in beaten egg, then into coating mixture. Bake 10–12 minutes at 400°.

CURRY DIP:

$^1/_2$ c ranch salad dressing
$^1/_4$ c orange marmalade

1 tsp curry
2–3 drops hot pepper
    sauce, if desired

Stir together. Refrigerate until ready to use.

Sauerkraut Balls

½ lb pork sausage meat
⅓ c onion, finely chopped
1 tbsp flour
14 oz canned sauerkraut,
   well drained, finely chopped
4 oz cream cheese, softened
1 tsp prepared mustard
1 tsp parsley flakes

⅛ tsp salt
¼ tsp garlic powder
¼ tsp pepper
⅓ c flour
2 large eggs
2 tbsp water
1 c fine bread crumbs
Fat, for deep frying

Fry sausage meat and onion in frying pan until no pink remains and onion is soft. Sprinkle flour over top; mix. Add sauerkraut, cream cheese, mustard, parsley, salt, garlic powder, and pepper. Stir until blended. Chill until it will hold its shape. Roll into 1-inch balls.

Put flour into one bowl, beaten eggs in another bowl, and bread crumbs in another. Roll balls first in flour, then in eggs, then in bread crumbs, until coated.

Carefully drop balls one at a time in hot oil or fat. Deep-fry until browned, about 3 minutes. Remove with slotted spoon to tray lined with paper towels to drain. Serve warm. Makes approximately 30.

Dried Garlic Spareribs

1 lb spareribs, chopped in
   1-inch squares
Pinch gourmet powder
2 tbsp Chinese cooking wine
2 tbsp light soy sauce
1 tbsp sugar

$\frac{1}{8}$ tsp salt or garlic
   salt
3–4 cloves minced
   garlic
Dash pepper
A few drops sesame
   oil

Marinate spareribs with 1 tablespoon cooking wine, 1 tablespoon soy sauce, and gourmet powder for 30 minutes. Deep-fry in hot oil for 5 minutes. Remove to a plate.

Using a hot wok, add 1 tablespoon peanut oil until almost smoky. Put in minced garlic to brown for a few seconds, then add spareribs, sugar, pepper, garlic salt, remainder of cooking wine and soy sauce, and sesame oil. Stir-fry for 3 minutes over medium heat. Serve.

Beverages

"I tell you the truth,
anyone who gives you a
cup of water in my name
because you belong to Christ
will certainly not lose his reward."

MARK 9:41

Fresh Berry Punch

1 (12-oz) bag fresh cranberries	1 can thawed pineapple juice
3 c water	concentrate
1 envelope raspberry	1 large banana, mashed
beverage mix	1 large bottle ginger ale

Puree 2 cups cranberries. Combine pureed cranberries, remaining whole cranberries, and water in large saucepan. Cook over high heat until cranberries begin to pop; remove from heat. Stir in remaining ingredients except ginger ale. Freeze about 12 hours, stir, and refreeze.

To serve:
Puree slush in food processor, spoon into pitcher, and mix in ginger ale.

Fruit Punch

10 c sugar	1 doz oranges
10 c water	1 can pineapple, grapefruit,
2 doz lemons	or grape juice

Make syrup of water, sugar, and rind of 3 lemons and 3 oranges. Boil 10 minutes. Cool, add fruit juices, and strain. Dilute as required.

Cranberry Juice

4 c cranberries
4 c water

$^2/_3$ c sugar or
1 c corn syrup

Cook cranberries until skins pop open. Strain through cheesecloth. Heat, add sugar, and boil for 2 minutes. Chill before serving. Lemon, orange, grapefruit, or pineapple juice may be combined with this.

Slush

1 (48-oz) can pineapple juice
1 (12-oz) can frozen orange juice
concentrate (thawed and
undiluted)

2 (6-oz) cans frozen
lemonade concentrate
(thawed and undiluted)

Mix all ingredients together and store in freezer in ice-cream pail. When serving, place slush in bottom of a tall glass and fill with 7-Up or ginger ale. Garnish with maraschino cherry.

Hot Cappuccino

1 c instant hot chocolate
   mix powder
½ c instant coffee granules
   (good quality)
½ c powdered nondairy
   coffee whitener
½ c skim milk powder

1¼ tsp ground
   cinnamon
¼ tsp ground
   nutmeg
Boiling water
Grated chocolate
   (optional)

Mix dry ingredients well. Use ¼ cup mixture for each 2 cups boiling water. Put desired amount in blender until foamy and pour into mugs. May be sprinkled with grated chocolate if desired.

Wassail Punch

2 qt apple cider
2 c orange juice
2 c pineapple juice
½ c lemon juice

½ c sugar
12 cloves, whole
4 cinnamon sticks,
   3–4" long

Bring all ingredients to a boil. Reduce heat. Simmer 10–15 minutes. Remove cloves and cinnamon sticks. Serve warm. Makes 3½ quarts.

Holiday Punch

2 c cranberry cocktail
4 c lemonade
1 c orange juice

Maraschino cherries
Lemon slices
3 (6-oz) bottles of
    ginger ale

Mix all ingredients (except ginger ale) together in a large bowl. Chill. Add ginger ale just before serving. Yields 18 punch cups.

Cranberry-Orange Punch

1 (6-oz) can frozen orange
    juice concentrate,
    reconstituted (3 c)

1¾ c cranberry juice
    cocktail, chilled
1 (12-oz) bottle
    ginger ale, chilled

Combine juices in large pitcher or small punch bowl with ice. Stir in ginger ale just before serving. Makes 6½ cups.

Three-Fruit Punch

1 (6-oz) can frozen lemonade
  concentrate
1 (10-oz) pkg frozen strawberries,
  thawed

1 (8-oz) can crushed
  pineapple
3 qt cold ginger ale
Crushed ice

Blend lemonade, pineapple, and strawberries until smooth (can be made in advance and refrigerated). Combine with ginger ale and ice. Makes 1 gallon.

Apple Juice Nog

3 c pure apple juice
3 eggs
2 c vanilla ice cream

¼ tsp cinnamon
Nutmeg

Combine all ingredients except nutmeg in blender container. Cover and blend until smooth, then chill. Pour into glasses and sprinkle with nutmeg.

Tahitian Punch

1 can pineapple juice, chilled
1 can orange-grapefruit juice,
  chilled
1 pt lemon or lime sherbet

2 qt carbonated lemon-lime
  beverage, chilled

In large punch bowl, stir together juices and carbonated beverage.
Spoon sherbet into bowl. Serve immediately. Garnish with citrus
slices and a sprig of mint if desired.

Golden Glow Punch

3 c unsweetened pineapple juice
3 large bottles 7-Up or ginger ale

1 qt orange juice
1 c lemon juice

Mix and serve with sliced oranges and maraschino cherries if
desired.

Spiced Tea

4 tea bags orange pekoe tea
Juice of 3 oranges and 3 lemons
4 tsp cinnamon

1½ tsp cloves
2 c sugar
1 gal water (16 c)

Simmer 20 minutes and remove tea bags.

Candies/ Confectioneries/ Sweets

Eat honey, my son, for it is good;
honey from the comb is sweet to your taste.

PROVERBS 24:13

Almond Florentine

Graham wafers
1 c butter
1 c brown sugar

1 c flaked almonds
Honey (optional)

Layer wafers on cookie sheet and set aside. Melt butter and brown sugar, add honey if desired, and cook over medium heat for 5 minutes—*Do not boil*. Spoon mixture over wafers. Sprinkle almonds on top. Bake at 350° for 10 minutes.

Christmas Fruit Balls

1 bag mini marshmallows
2 c graham wafer crumbs
½ c red maraschino cherries, halved

½ c green maraschino cherries, halved
1 (15-oz) can sweetened condensed milk
½ c walnuts, chopped

Mix together everything but the coconut. Chill overnight. Shape chilled mixture into balls which are about 1 inch in diameter, then roll in coconut. Store in a covered container in refrigerator. Makes 4 dozen balls.

Peppermint Jells

1 box Certo Crystals powdered
   fruit pectin
³/₄ c water
¹/₂ tsp baking soda

1 c icing sugar
1 c light corn syrup
10 drops green food coloring
¹/₂ tsp peppermint extract
¹/₂ c icing sugar

Mix pectin, water, and soda (mixture will foam slightly) in a 2-quart saucepan. In separate pan, mix sugar and corn syrup. Heat both mixtures at the same time, stirring constantly until foam has disappeared from pectin mixture and sugar mixture is boiling rapidly (3–5 minutes). Pour pectin mixture in a slow steady stream into sugar mixture, stirring constantly. Be careful and use a long-handled spoon; this superboils at the time the 2 liquids are mixed. Boil and stir 1 minute longer. Remove from heat and stir in coloring and flavoring. Pour into 9¹/₂x5¹/₄-inch loaf pan or 8x8-inch square pan. Let stand at room temperature until cool and firm. Cut into ³/₄-inch squares and roll in icing sugar. Let stand at room temperature overnight.

VARIATIONS:

CINNAMON: 15 drops red food coloring, 4 drops cinnamon or
   cassia oil
ORANGE: 10 drops orange food coloring, 1¹/₂ to 2 tsp orange
   extract

Just Like an O'Henry Bar

12 oz chocolate chips
12 oz butterscotch chips

2 c dry Chinese chow-mein
noodles
2 c unsalted peanuts

Melt the chocolate in double boiler and add the rest of the ingredients. Drop on waxed paper and refrigerate.

Caramel Creams

3 c white sugar
1 c corn syrup

1 c sweet cream

Boil gently 10–15 minutes or until a small quantity dropped in cold water forms a firm ball. Beat until thick and cool enough to handle.

There are 3 options to shape/finish.

Roll in small balls and dip in melted semisweet chocolate; add 3–4 drops oil of peppermint, pour into pan, and cut into squares; or shape into cylinders about 1 inch in diameter, roll in chopped pecans, and slice.

Christmas Fudge

3 c sugar
½ c boiling water (for
    colored fudge, use the
    liquid from the cherries)
½ c corn syrup

2 egg whites
1 tsp vanilla
1 small bottle green
    or red cherries,
    cut fine

Combine syrup, sugar, and water. Boil until syrup forms hard ball when dropped on ice. Pour gradually over egg whites which have been beaten stiff. Continue beating until mixture holds shape. Add cherries during beating. Pour into buttered pan and cut when cool.

Chocolate Snowballs

Note: This sounds strange, but they are delicious!
No one will ever know what they're made of!

1 medium hot mashed potato
2–3 c icing sugar
Vanilla

Chocolate
Coconut or chopped
    nuts

Mix 1 cup icing sugar into the mashed potato; add vanilla. Mix in additional icing sugar until it makes a soft dough. Roll into balls and let set. Dip in melted chocolate and roll in coconut or chopped nuts.

Maple Crisps

1 c shortening
2 c brown sugar, packed
1 tsp maple extract
2 eggs
3½ c flour

¼ tsp salt
1 tsp soda
1 c almonds,
    blanched and
    chopped

Cream shortening, sugar, and maple extract. Add eggs and mix well. Add flour, salt, and soda. Mix in almonds; combine thoroughly. Roll or cut cookies. Bake at 400° for 6–8 minutes. Store in loosely covered tin to keep crisp.

Porcupines

1 c dates, chopped
1 c nuts, chopped
1½ c coconut, plus extra for
    rolling

1 c brown sugar
1 tbsp butter
2 eggs
1 tsp vanilla

Mix dates, nuts, and coconut. Blend in butter, eggs, and vanilla. Roll into balls, then roll in additional coconut. Bake at 325° for 18–20 minutes. Makes 5 dozen.

Christmas Soft Candies

1 can Eagle Brand milk
2 lb icing sugar
Flavoring—pick one of peppermint,
　　almond, maple, or vanilla—or
　　divide dough for a variety

Nuts, dates, or cherries
6 squares semisweet or
　　unsweetened chocolate
1½ tbsp paraffin wax

Mix canned milk and icing sugar to make a dough. Either mix the entire batch with one type of flavoring, or divide for a variety. Add nuts, dates, or cherries to the base and roll into tiny balls. Set to cool. Melt wax and chocolate in double boiler. Using a toothpick, dip in candies to coat. Put on cookie sheet to harden.

Snookie Cookies

½ c broken walnuts
½ c dates
½ lb colored marshmallows,
　　cut into pieces

½ c unsweetened
　　condensed milk
¼ c boiling water
2½ c graham wafer crumbs

Mix first 4 ingredients and pour boiling water over them. Stir in wafer crumbs. Make into a roll about 2 inches thick. Let stand overnight. Cut into slices.

Quick Chocolate Drops

3 c quick oats
1 c shredded coconut
6 tbsp cocoa
$\frac{1}{2}$ c butter

$\frac{1}{2}$ c milk
2 c white sugar
$\frac{1}{2}$ tsp vanilla

Mix oats, coconut, and cocoa. Heat butter, milk, and sugar together in a saucepan until almost to the boiling point, but do not boil. Pour over dry mixture and stir well. Drop by spoonfuls onto buttered waxed paper. Chill until firm.

Brigadeiras

(pronounced Brig-uh-DAY-ruz)

1 can sweetened condensed milk
4 tbsp butter or margarine
2 tbsp cocoa or Nesquik
Sugar, chocolate, or colored sprinkles

Melt butter in a pan. Add other ingredients and cook over medium heat. Cook and stir constantly until really thick—about 5 or 10 minutes—until you see the bottom of the pan easily. Let cool. Roll into balls quickly. Then roll in sugar, chocolate, or colored sprinkles. Makes 2–3 dozen.

Peanut Butter Fudge

¾ c butter or 1½ sticks
   margarine
3 c sugar
1 (5-oz) can or ⅔ c
   evaporated milk
½ pkg (about 5 oz)
   peanut butter chips

½ pkg (about 6 oz)
   semisweet chocolate
   chips
1 (7-oz) jar
   marshmallow creme
1 tsp vanilla

Lightly grease 13x9-inch or 9-inch square pan. Mix margarine, sugar, and milk in a heavy saucepan. Bring to full, rolling boil over medium heat, stirring constantly. Continue boiling for 5 minutes on medium heat, stirring constantly to prevent scorching. Remove from heat. Gradually stir in chips until melted. Add marshmallow creme and vanilla. Mix well. Pour into prepared pan. Cool at room temperature. Cut into squares.

No-Bake Christmas Graham Fudge

1 (12-oz) pkg semisweet
   chocolate chips
1/4 c butter or margarine
2 1/2 c graham cracker crumbs

1 1/2 c almonds or pecans,
   chopped
1 (14-oz) can sweetened
   condensed milk
1 tsp vanilla

Melt chocolate chips and butter together until smooth. In large bowl, combine graham crumbs and nuts. Stir in condensed milk and vanilla until crumbs are moistened, then stir in chocolate mixture until mixed. Pat evenly in greased 12x8-inch pan. Let stand at room temperature 2 hours before cutting.

Toffee

1 c butter
1 1/4 c brown sugar
3 tbsp corn syrup

3 tbsp water
1 1/2 c whole almonds
Chocolate chips, to taste

Bake almonds at 375° for 10 minutes on baking sheet. Turn off and leave in oven.

Cook first 4 ingredients over medium heat stirring constantly until mixture reaches 300° (hard crack) on candy thermometer.

Spread candy on cookie sheet with nuts (work fast). Cool. Melt chocolate chips; drizzle or coat to taste. Crack.

Cookies

Nehemiah said,
"Go and enjoy choice food and sweet drinks,
and send some to
those who have nothing prepared.
This day is sacred to our Lord.
Do not grieve,
for the joy of the LORD is your strength."

NEHEMIAH 8:10

Merry Fruit Cookies

1½ c mixed fruit, glazed
2 eggs
½ c dates, chopped
¼ c flour
¾ c dark raisins
½ lb butter

1 c sugar
½ tsp almond flavoring
½ tsp baking powder
½ tsp baking soda
½ tsp ground cinnamon
2¼ c flour

Place fruit, raisins, dates, and ¼ cup flour in bowl; stir to coat fruit with flour. Cream margarine and sugar in another bowl. Add eggs one at a time, beating well after each addition. Add flavoring. Stir dry ingredients; add fruit mixture and stir. Add to batter. Stir until it is too difficult to mix. Work with hands until flour is mixed in. Shape into 2 or 3 logs about 1½ inches in diameter. Roll each log in waxed paper and chill for 1 hour or longer. Cut into ¼-inch slices. Arrange ½ inch apart; bake at 375° for 10 minutes until golden. Makes 4–5 dozen.

Snickerdoodles

2 c sugar
2 eggs, well beaten
½ c butter, softened
1 tsp vanilla
4 c flour

4 tsp baking powder
1 tsp salt
1 c milk
1 c raisins
Cinnamon and sugar for
garnish

Gradually add sugar to eggs. Stir in butter and mix well. Add vanilla. Mix dry ingredients and add alternately to the egg mixture with the milk, beating well between additions. Stir in raisins. Drop by tea-spoonfuls onto a greased cookie sheet, about an inch apart. Sprinkle with cinnamon and sugar. Bake 10–12 minutes at 375°.

Cherry Christmas Cookies

1 c soft butter
¾ c brown sugar
½ tsp vanilla
⅛ tsp salt

2½ c flour
1 c sliced almonds
½ c red cherries, whole
½ c green cherries, whole

Cream butter, add sugar and then vanilla, salt, and flour. Finally, add nuts and cherries and form into rolls. Leave in fridge overnight. Slice thinly with a sharp knife and bake on greased baking sheet at 375° for 10 minutes.

Cracker Jack Cookies

1 c butter
1 c white sugar
1 c brown sugar
2 tsp vanilla
1½ c flour
1 tsp baking powder

1 tsp baking soda
2 c oatmeal
1 c coconut
2 c Rice Krispies
2 eggs

Cream butter; add sugar, eggs, and vanilla and cream well. Combine dry ingredients and mix all together. Stir in oatmeal, coconut, and Rice Krispies by hand. Drop by teaspoonfuls onto greased cookie sheet. Bake at 350° for 10–12 minutes until nicely browned.

Shortbread

1 lb butter
1 c icing sugar
1 c cornstarch

3 c flour
Pinch of salt
A few drops of lemon juice

Cream butter; gradually add remaining ingredients, but do not over-beat. Press cookies onto ungreased baking sheet, using a cookie press. Bake at 275° for approximately 25 minutes, or until just slightly brown at bottom.

Hazelnut Meringue Cookies

2 egg whites
$^1/_2$ c granulated sugar
$^1/_2$ tsp vanilla

$^1/_2$ tsp vinegar
$^1/_8$ tsp salt
1 c hazelnuts

Line baking sheets with either brown paper or parchment paper. Beat egg whites until soft peaks form. Gradually add sugar and salt; continue beating for 3–4 minutes until meringue is very stiff and sugar has dissolved. Beat in vanilla and vinegar. Fold in hazelnuts.

Drop by spoonfuls in small mounds (about $1^1/_2$ inches) on prepared baking sheets. Bake in 300° oven for 30 minutes or until light brown. Turn off heat. Leave in oven until oven is cool or overnight to thoroughly dry. Lift off paper. Makes 24 cookies.

Cherry Flips

1 c butter
½ c icing sugar
2 egg yolks
2 c sifted cake flour
¼ tsp salt

2 tsp almond flavoring
30 maraschino cherries
    (save juice)
Crushed nuts or
    shredded coconut

Cream butter and sugar; add egg yolks and beat well. Blend in flour and salt; add flavoring. Pinch off pieces and roll out flat in your hand. Insert a cherry and fold the dough around it to form a ball. Bake on a greased baking sheet at 325° for 25 minutes or until light brown.

When cold, dip in thin icing made from 1½ cups icing sugar and ½ cup cherry juice. Roll in nuts or coconut.

Candy Cane Sugar Cookies

1 c sugar
1 c butter, softened
½ c milk
1 egg
1 tsp vanilla
1 tsp almond extract

3½ c flour
1 tsp baking powder
¼ tsp salt
½ tsp red food coloring
Crushed candy canes, to taste

Mix sugar, butter, milk, egg, vanilla, and almond extract. Stir in flour, baking powder, and salt. Divide dough in half. Tint one-half with red food coloring. Cover and refrigerate at least 4 hours.

One at a time, roll both colors into ropes. Press 1 white and 1 pink rope together, then twist together. Cut into 8-inch lengths, then curl one end over to make the shape of a candy cane, being careful not to let the dough "break" as you make the shape. Sprinkle with crushed candy canes; bake at 375° for 9–12 minutes. Do not overbake.

VARIATION: Tint one-half green, twist, and join ropes into circles to make wreaths. Decorate with cut maraschino cherries.

Christmas Macaroons

3 egg whites
1 c fine granulated sugar
1 tbsp cornstarch
Pinch of salt
1 c coconut

$^1/_2$ c candied cherries,
   cut into pieces
$^1/_4$ c almonds, blanched
   and cut into pieces

Beat the egg whites until stiff but not dry. Mix sugar, salt, and cornstarch and add gradually, beating constantly. Cook in a double boiler until a crust forms. Remove from heat. Fold in fruit and nuts. Roll into small balls. Bake on well-greased baking sheet at 300° until firm and slightly brown, about 20–30 minutes. Makes about 3 dozen.

Dips

" 'Bring the fattened calf and kill it.
Let's have a feast and celebrate.' "

LUKE 15:23

Imitation Crab Dip

1 c sour cream
1 c mayonnaise
1 pkg Knorr vegetable soup

1 (6-oz) can water
   chestnuts, drained
   and chopped
6–8 oz imitation crab

Mix and chill overnight. Serve with crackers.

Crab Dip

8 oz cream cheese
2 tsp mayonnaise
2 tsp Worcestershire sauce
1 small onion, grated

2 tsp lemon juice
1 bottle Heinz chili sauce
1 can crabmeat
Parsley flakes

Mix first 5 ingredients until smooth. Spread in pan. Pour chili sauce over. Drain crab. Spread over. Sprinkle with parsley. Set in refrigerator at least 3 hours; serve with crackers.

Taco Dip

4 oz cream cheese

Spread over 13-inch plate.

LAYER THE FOLLOWING ON TOP:

1 lb cooked ground beef
1 pkg sour cream
1 envelope taco seasoning
1 can tomato paste
1 tomato, chopped

2–3 green onions
Shredded cheddar cheese, to taste
Chopped lettuce, to taste

Serve with taco chips.

Party Ham Spread

BLEND AND CHILL:

2 cans flaked ham
½ c mayonnaise
2 hard-boiled eggs

2 tbsp minced onion
¼ c relish

Serve with party crackers.

Mexican Dip

1 lb cooked ground beef
1/2 c green pepper, chopped
2 cloves garlic, chopped
1 onion, chopped

1 pkg taco seasoning
1 can refried beans
1 1/2 c mild salsa
2–3 c shredded cheese
Taco chips or taco
    shells

Preheat oven to 350°. Fry beef in a skillet and drain. Add onion, green pepper, and garlic. Simmer 10 minutes. Spread refried beans over 9x13-inch casserole dish. Spread beef mixture on top, then sour cream. Top with cheese. Bake for 35 minutes or until browned. Serve with taco chips or roll in soft taco shells.

Shrimp Spread

1 can tiny shrimp
1 (4-oz) pkg cream cheese,
    softened

1 clove garlic, minced
Lemon juice
Cayenne pepper

Coarsely chop the shrimp. Add the cream cheese, a few drops of lemon juice, and garlic to taste. Mix, cover, and chill. Sprinkle with cayenne pepper and serve with crackers.

Easy Taco Dip

1 (8-oz) pkg cream cheese,
  softened

1 c sour cream
1 pkg dry taco mix,
  or to taste

Combine ingredients and spread in shallow, round dish.

Combine 1 cup each: chopped iceberg lettuce and chopped tomatoes, drained. Top with chopped green onions and shredded cheddar cheese. Serve with taco chips.

Shrimp Mold

1 envelope gelatin
$\frac{1}{2}$ c tomato soup, undiluted
1 can shrimp pieces
$\frac{1}{2}$ c celery, cut fine
$\frac{1}{4}$ c green onions, cut fine

$\frac{3}{4}$ c mayonnaise or salad
  dressing
1 (8-oz) pkg cream
  cheese, softened

Dissolve gelatin in 2 tablespoons cold water. Heat tomato soup and mix together. Add balance of ingredients, mix, and pour into mold or plastic bowl. Let set overnight. Serve with crackers.

Fresh Vegetables with Savory Dip

Fresh vegetables
1 (4-oz) pkg of cream
   cheese, softened
2 tbsp milk
½ tsp Dijon mustard
½ tsp dried Italian seasoning

1 tbsp parsley, chopped
   or 1 tsp dried parsley
   flakes
1 small clove garlic,
   minced

Combine all ingredients except vegetables and spoon into small serving bowl. Prepare a variety of vegetables. Place dip in center of platter and surround with vegetables.

Easy Cracker Dip

LAYER IN ROUND DISH:

1 (8-oz) pkg cream cheese,
   softened
1 small jar cocktail sauce

1 can small shrimp or
   crabmeat

Serve with crackers.

Spinach Dip

1 pkg frozen spinach,
  (uncooked)
2 c sour cream
1 c mayonnaise

1 pkg Knorr vegetable soup
1 can water chestnuts
$1/3$ c green onions, chopped
1 large pumpernickel bread

Dry and finely chop spinach. Drain water chestnuts and finely chop. Blend all ingredients together. Cut off top of pumpernickel bread and scoop out inside. Fill with dip. Use top and inside of bread as well as crackers and vegetables for dipping.

Christmas Party Shrimp Spread

1 can broken shrimp
1 (8-oz) pkg cream cheese,
  softened
2 tbsp mayonnaise
1 tbsp ketchup

$1/2$ tsp prepared mustard
Dash of garlic powder
  (optional)
Chopped celery or green
  onions (optional)

Cream the cream cheese, mayonnaise, ketchup, mustard, and garlic powder. Add mashed and drained shrimp; mix well. Add garlic, celery, and/or green onions if desired. Refrigerate.

Cheese Ball

1 (8-oz) pkg cream cheese, softened
2½ c sharp cheddar cheese, grated
½ c dill pickles, chopped
½ c walnuts, finely chopped

¼ c green onions, finely chopped
2 tbsp Miracle Whip or mayonnaise
1 tsp Worcestershire sauce
Pinch of parsley, basil, and dill

Combine all the above except walnuts and spices, beating until smooth. Cover and chill until firm. Shape into a ball and roll into a mixture of walnuts, parsley, basil, and dill.

Low-Calorie Veggie Dip

1 c plain yogurt
¼ tsp salt
¼ tsp dill weed
⅛ tsp garlic salt

3 green onions, finely chopped
Dash of pepper
1 tsp honey

Combine all ingredients. Chill and serve with crackers.

Blue Cheese & Sun-Dried Tomato Spread

1 (8-oz) pkg cream cheese, room temperature
1/4 c sun-dried tomatoes in oil, drained, finely chopped
1/4 c crumbled blue cheese
1/4 c fresh parsley, chopped
1/4 c green pepper, finely chopped
1 tsp oregano
1 clove garlic, minced
Dash of freshly ground pepper

Combine all ingredients. Chill and serve with crackers or cocktail rye bread.

Cool Yogurt Dip

1 c plain low-fat yogurt
1/2 c grated cucumber, with peel
1/4–1/2 tsp salt
2 tbsp chopped fresh mint leaves, packed
1/4 tsp granulated sugar

Combine all ingredients and let stand at room temperature for 1 hour to meld flavors. Serve.

Tangy Cheese Spread

2 c finely shredded old
   cheddar cheese
Dash of garlic salt
1 tsp Dijon mustard

1 (4-oz) pkg cream
   cheese, softened
Dash of Tabasco sauce
Dash of Worcestershire
   sauce
$1/4$ c dry sherry

Using food processor or mixer, combine cheddar cheese, garlic salt, and Dijon mustard. Add cream cheese and blend until smooth. Add Tabasco, Worcestershire, and sherry. Beat until creamy. Spoon into serving dish; cover and chill for several days to blend flavors. Serve at room temperature with crackers.

Seafood Cracker Spread

1 (8-oz) pkg cream cheese
2 tbsp Thousand Island salad
   dressing
1 tin crabmeat

$1/4$–$1/2$ bottle chili sauce
   or seafood cocktail
   sauce
1 can shrimp

Mix cream cheese and salad dressing and spread on inner circle of dinner plate. Pour sauce over top. Crumble crab and shrimp meat and sprinkle on top. Serve with crackers.

Hot Crab Delight

1 (8-oz) pkg cream cheese at
   room temperature
1 (6½-oz) tin crabmeat
2 tbsp green onion, chopped
½ tsp horseradish

½ c slivered almonds
1 tbsp milk
½ tsp salt
1 tbsp lemon juice
Dash of pepper

Combine all ingredients except almonds; mix well. Garnish with almonds. Warm in oven at 350° for 20 minutes. Serve as a dip with crackers.

Surprise Spread

1 (8-oz) pkg cream cheese,
   softened

¼ c mayonnaise
½ c sour cream

Mix together and spread over a pizza pan-style plate.

ADD:

Woodman's Tangy Seafood
   Sauce
2 cans shrimp
2 c grated mozzarella cheese

1 c green peppers,
   chopped
3 green onions, chopped
1 tomato, diced

Sprinkle over cream mixture. Dip with crackers.

Homestyle Boursin

2 (8-oz) pkg softened cream
   cheese
1/4 c mayonnaise
2 tsp Dijon mustard

1 clove garlic, minced
2 tbsp chives, finely chopped
2 tbsp fresh dill, finely
   chopped

Beat cheese, mayonnaise, mustard, chives, dill, and garlic with a mixer in a large bowl until thoroughly blended. Spoon into a small serving bowl or line a 2-cup mold with aluminum foil and spoon in mixture. Cover and refrigerate overnight. Turn out onto a small serving plate and peel off foil. Serve with crackers and vegetable dippers—celery sticks, cucumber slices, cherry tomatoes, zucchini, broccoli, and cauliflower florets.

Spicy Vegetable Dip

1 c sour cream
1 c mayonnaise
1/2 c chili sauce
1 tsp horseradish

1 tsp HP sauce or your
   favorite spicy steak
   sauce
1 tsp minced onion

Mix and serve.

Layered Bean Dip

2 (14-oz) cans refried beans
1 (4-oz) can green chiles, chopped
1 envelope taco seasoning mix
2 ripe avocados, peeled and pitted
2 jars taco sauce, mild, medium, or hot

2 tbsp lemon juice
1½ c sour cream
3 c shredded lettuce
1½ c shredded cheddar cheese
Black olives, sliced (optional)

Mix together refried beans, chiles, and taco seasoning. Spread on a 12-inch serving platter. Blend avocados, lemon juice, and ½ cup taco sauce until smooth and spread on top of bean mixture. Spread sour cream on top of avocado mixture. Top with lettuce, cheese, remaining taco sauce, and olives if desired. Serve with taco chips.

Squares

They are more precious than gold,
than much pure gold;
they are sweeter than honey,
than honey from the comb.

PSALM 19:10

Butter Tart Squares

BASE:

1 c flour   ½ c butter
¼ c white sugar

Combine flour and sugar. Cut in butter until crumbly. Press into 9-inch pan. Bake at 350° for 15 minutes.

TOPPING:

2 tbsp butter, melted   ½ tsp vanilla
2 eggs   Pinch salt
1 c brown sugar   1 c raisins
2 tbsp flour   ½ c walnuts
½ tbsp baking powder

Mix together butter and eggs; blend in sugar, flour, baking powder, vanilla, and salt. Stir in raisins and walnuts. Pour over base. Bake at 350° for 20–30 minutes or until top springs back when touched lightly. Cool before cutting into squares.

Dream Slice

BASE:

½ c butter
1 c flour

Pinch of salt
2 tbsp brown sugar

Spread on 8x8-inch pan. Bake at 350° for 15 minutes.

TOPPING:

2 beaten eggs
1½ c brown sugar
4 tbsp flour
½ tsp baking powder

1 c walnuts, chopped
½ c coconut
½ c glazed cherries

Mix and pour on base; bake 20 minutes longer at 300°.

Peanut Butter-Marshmallow Slice

½ c butter
1 c peanut butter

2 (6-oz) pkg butterscotch
   chips
4 c miniature marshmallows

Melt first 3 ingredients in double boiler, then add marshmallows.
Pour into greased 8x8-inch pan. Keep in refrigerator.

Maple Pecan Squares

BASE:

1 c flour

¼ c brown sugar
½ c butter

TOPPING:

⅔ c brown sugar
1 c maple syrup
2 eggs beaten
½ c soft butter

¼ tsp salt
⅔ c pecan halves
½ tsp vanilla
2 tbsp flour

Preheat oven to 350°. Rub flour, sugar, and butter together. Press mixture firmly into 7x11-inch pan. Bake at 350° for 5 minutes. Note: It should not be completely cooked. Combine sugar and syrup in a saucepan. Simmer 5 minutes. Cool lightly. Pour over beaten eggs, stirring. Stir in remaining ingredients. Spread over partially baked dough. Bake at 450° for 10 minutes then reduce heat to 350° for 20 minutes. Cool and cut into squares.

Cherry Slice

Graham wafers

1 pt whipped cream

1 pkg mini marshmallows

1 can cherry pie filling

Whip the cream, add mini marshmallows. Pour half of this mixture on wafers. Spread with pie filling. Pour remainder of cream mixture on top of cherries. Crumble 6 wafers and sprinkle on top. Refrigerate until serving.

Rocky Road Squares

BASE:

4 squares unsweetened chocolate

$^{3}/_{4}$ c butter

$1^{1}/_{2}$ c sugar

3 eggs

1 tbsp milk

1 c flour

1 c nuts, chopped

Heat chocolate and butter over low heat until butter melts. Stir until smooth, then stir in sugar. Mix in eggs and milk until well blended. Stir in flour and nuts. Spread in greased 9-inch square pan. Bake at 350° for 40 minutes. Add Rocky Road Topping and bake 10 minutes longer.

ROCKY ROAD TOPPING:

2 c miniature marshmallows

1 c semisweet chocolate chips

1 c nuts, chopped

Jam Bars

¹/₂ c butter
1 tbsp sugar
1 egg, beaten

1 c flour
1 tsp baking powder
Pinch salt

Mix and put in pan spread with jam.

TOPPING:

1 rounded tbsp butter
³/₄ c sugar
1 egg

1¹/₂ c coconut or crushed
    cornflakes
1 tsp vanilla

Beat sugar and butter together, add beaten egg, then stir in dry ingredients. Spread over top of base mixture. Bake 20–30 minutes or until top is nicely browned and thick.

Krispy Krunch Bars

2 c peanut butter
2¹/₂ c icing sugar
2¹/₂ c crisp rice cereal

¹/₄ c butter or margarine
¹/₂ c walnuts, chopped
    (optional)

ICING:

²/₃ c semisweet chocolate chips   1 tsp butter

Mix all ingredients except icing together in bowl. Press into 9x9-inch pan lined with waxed paper. Melt together chocolate chips and butter and spread on top. Makes 36 bars.

Butterscotch Oat Squares

2 c quick or instant oats
1 c brown sugar, packed
$^1/_2$ c melted butter

$^1/_2$ tsp vanilla
Melted chocolate (optional)

Combine oats and brown sugar. Mix well. Add melted butter and vanilla. Mix thoroughly. Divide mixture evenly into 2 ungreased 8-inch square pans. Spread and pat evenly. Bake at 375° for about 10 minutes or until golden. Squares will be soft but harden on cooling. Can be drizzled with melted chocolate, if desired. Allow to cool 5 minutes, then mark in squares with sharp knife. Loosen edges and allow to cool before removing from pans.

Brownies

1 c butter or margarine
4 tbsp cocoa
$1^1/_2$ c sugar
1 c flour

2 tsp baking powder
1 tsp vanilla
4 eggs
1 c walnuts, chopped

Melt butter or margarine in saucepan. Add cocoa, sugar, flour, baking powder, and walnuts. Add eggs one at a time, beating in well after each addition. Pour into greased 9x13-inch baking pan. Bake at 350° for 25–30 minutes. Ice with your favorite icing or sprinkle top with sifted icing sugar.

Almond Bars

1 c flour   ½ c butter
2 tbsp icing sugar

Press into a 9x9-inch pan. Bake at 350° for 15 minutes.

In double boiler, boil for 3 minutes:
4 tbsp butter   1 tsp vanilla
½ c brown sugar   ¼ c cream

Remove and add 1 cup sliced almonds, then spoon over base. Bake 15 minutes more.

Puffed Wheat Squares/Balls

½ c butter   1 tsp vanilla
½ c corn syrup   8 c puffed wheat for
1 c brown sugar   balls, 9 c for
2 tbsp cocoa   squares

In large pot, melt butter on medium heat and then add corn syrup, brown sugar, and cocoa and mix well. Increase heat slightly and once mixture starts to boil, let boil for only 30 seconds. Turn heat off and add the vanilla, then puffed wheat. Mix well to coat puffed wheat. Roll into balls or press into buttered 9x13-inch pan. Once cooled, cut into squares.

Date Square/Matrimonial Cake

¾ c butter
1 c brown sugar
½ tsp nutmeg
Milk

1 tsp baking soda
1½ c oatmeal
1½ c flour

DATE FILLING:

2 c dates, chopped
½ c brown sugar
1 c warm water

A little lemon juice
to taste, if
desired, for more
flavor

Rub butter into dry ingredients. Add enough milk to hold together. Reserve ½ cup crumbs. Pack the remainder in 8x8-inch cake pan, spread with the date filling, top with the reserve crumbs, and bake at 325–350° for 25–35 minutes.

Nanaimo Bars

Base:

½ c butter
¼ c sugar
1 egg, beaten
4 tbsp cocoa

2 c graham wafer crumbs
½ c coconut
1 c nuts, chopped

Mix first 4 ingredients in a saucepan and cook until smooth. Add remaining ingredients, mix, and press into 8x8-inch pan. Bake at 350° for 10 minutes or until slightly golden. Cool.

Middle Layer:

¼ c butter
2 tbsp custard powder

3 tbsp milk
2 c icing sugar

Beat until smooth and spread on top of cooled base.

Top Layer:

4 squares semisweet chocolate   1 tsp butter

Melt together and pour on top.

Magic Cookie Bars

½ c margarine or butter
1½ c graham cracker
    crumbs
1 (14-oz) can sweetened
    condensed milk (not evaporated)

1 (6-oz) pkg semisweet
    chocolate chips
1⅓ c flaked coconut
1 c nuts, chopped

Preheat oven to 350° or 325° for glass dish. In 9x13-inch baking pan, melt margarine in oven. Sprinkle crumbs over margarine, mix together, and press into pan. Pour condensed milk evenly over crumbs. Top evenly with remaining ingredients. Press down firmly. Bake 25–30 minutes or until lightly browned. Cool thoroughly before cutting.

Tarts

"If you come with us,
we will share with you
whatever good things the LORD gives us."

NUMBERS 10:32

Lemon Tart

2 c sugar
1/4 lb butter
Tart shells, baked

2 lemons, rind and juice
4 eggs

Melt butter and sugar in double boiler. Add rind, then beaten eggs and lemon juice. Boil to thicken. Place in baked tart shells. Cool.

Coconut Tarts

1 egg
1/2 c sugar
Pinch salt
Tart shells, unbaked

1 tbsp butter
1 1/2 c coconut
2 tbsp strawberry jam

Melt butter; add egg and beat well. Add sugar and pinch salt. Blend well. Mix in coconut. Put a drop of jam into each pastry shell; top with a spoon of above mixture. Bake at 350° for 15–20 minutes or until golden brown.

Crab Tarts

Tart shells, unbaked
4 eggs
2 c cream
⅓ c minced onion
1 tsp salt
Dash cayenne pepper

1 can crabmeat, drain and
    pat dry with a paper towel
1 c shredded Swiss or
    mozzarella cheese
Dried parsley flakes, to taste

Beat eggs until blended; stir in cream. Add onion, salt, and pepper. Set aside.

Sprinkle crabmeat and cheese into the tart shells. Pour egg mixture on top. Sprinkle with parsley. Bake at 375° until knife inserted comes out clean, approximately 15–20 minutes.

Vegetables

*Better a meal of vegetables
where there is love
than a fattened calf with hatred.*

PROVERBS 15:17

Hot Artichoke Spread

1 can artichokes, chopped
1 can green chiles, chopped
1 tomato, chopped

$^3/_4$ c Parmesan, reserve
$^1/_4$ c for top
1 c mayonnaise

Combine all ingredients. Bake in oven 350° for 20 minutes, or microwave on high for 4–5 minutes.

Crispy Zucchini Strips

3 zucchini
$^1/_3$ c flour
1 egg
1 tbsp water

$^1/_2$ c cornflake crumbs
$^1/_2$ tsp seasoned salt
$^1/_4$ c vegetable oil
$^1/_4$ c butter

Remove tips from zucchini but do not peel. Cut lengthwise into eighths. Cut each strip in half. Coat strips with flour. In shallow dish, beat together egg and water. In separate shallow dish, combine cornflake crumbs and seasoned salt. Dip each strip into egg wash then into seasoned crumbs, coating evenly.

In large skillet, heat half the oil and butter. Add half the zucchini strips and fry for 4–5 minutes, turning as needed to brown evenly. Remove strips to warm oven (200°). Cook remaining strips in remaining oil and butter.

Vegetable Pizza

Pillsbury croissant dough

Press into ungreased pizza pan and pinch sections together. Brown in 350° oven and cool thoroughly.

MIX:

1 (8-oz) pkg cream cheese	Dash garlic powder
1/2 c mayonnaise	Dill weed, to taste
Vegetables	

Top with shredded or nicely broken-up cauliflower, broccoli, carrots, and onions. Top with mozzarella cheese.

Miscellaneous

*Command them to do good,
to be rich in good deeds,
and to be generous and willing to share.*

1 Timothy 6:18

Nuts and Bolts

2 c Cheerios
2 c Crispix
2 c Shreddies
2 c pretzels

4–5 tbsp butter or margarine
2 tsp Worcestershire sauce
1½ tsp onion powder
1½ tsp garlic or seasoning salt

Melt butter or margarine. Add Worcestershire sauce and spices. Combine all other ingredients in large microwave-safe dish. Add melted mixture and stir well. Microwave on high 4–5 minutes, stirring twice. Cool.

Cheese Chips

½ tsp salt
¼ tsp paprika
1½ c flour
A few grains cayenne
½ c shortening

¾ c grated cheese
Cold water
Milk
Poppy or celery seeds

Combine dry ingredients; cut in shortening. Add cheese. Add enough water to hold ingredients together. Form in roll 1½ inches in diameter. Wrap in waxed paper and chill in refrigerator overnight. Slice thinly. Brush tops with milk and sprinkle with poppy or celery seeds. Bake at 400° until golden; time depends on amount of water used.

Gingerbread for Houses

⅓ c soft shortening	2 tsp soda
1 c brown sugar, packed	1 tsp salt
1½ c molasses	1½ tsp ginger
⅔ c cold water	1 tsp cloves
1 tsp vanilla	1 tsp cinnamon
7 c all-purpose flour,	¼ tsp allspice
sifted	¼ tsp nutmeg

Combine shortening, sugar, and molasses, and beat until well blended. Stir in water and vanilla. Sift flour, soda, salt, and spices together into mixture and blend thoroughly. Chill several hours or overnight.

Roll and cook on a baking sheet at 350° for 8–10 minutes. When completely cool, construct into Gingerbread House, holding it together with Decorative Icing.

DECORATIVE ICING:

3 egg whites	1 c icing sugar, sifted
¼ tsp cream of tartar	

Beat egg whites and cream of tartar until frothy. Add sugar gradually, beating well after each addition. Continue beating until very stiff and glossy. If it begins to get too soft when you are working with it, beat it again with mixer at high speed until firm.

Cheesy Grapes

4 oz cream cheese
$\frac{1}{4}$ c crumbled blue cheese
1 tbsp mayonnaise (approx)
1 clove minced garlic
   (optional)

$\frac{1}{4}$ tsp ground ginger
60 small, firm seedless
   grapes
2 c ground almonds,
   toasted

(To toast almonds, bake on baking sheet at 350° for 5 minutes or until golden.)

In bowl, cream together cheeses and mayonnaise, adding up to 1 tablespoon more mayonnaise for spreading consistency. Stir in garlic, if using, and ginger. Wash grapes and dry on paper towels. Stir grapes into cheese mixture, stirring gently to coat each grape thoroughly, rolling by hand if necessary to completely cover each grape. Roll cheese-covered grapes individually in almonds until coated. Place on flat platter or tray. Cover with plastic wrap and refrigerate for about 1 hour or up to 3 days. Makes 60.

Cheese Straws

$^1/_2$ tsp salt
$^1/_2$ tsp powdered ginger
1 c flour
1 c shredded sharp cheddar
   cheese, about 4 oz

$^1/_3$ c butter or margarine
$^1/_4$ c sesame seed, toasted
$^1/_2$ tsp Worcestershire sauce
2–2$^1/_2$ tsp cold water

Mix salt, ginger, and flour. Cut in butter with a pastry blender. Lightly stir in cheese and sesame seed. Mix Worcestershire sauce with 1 tablespoon of the water and sprinkle over flour; toss with a fork. Add remaining water while tossing, until moistened. Gather up with fingers to form a ball. On a lightly floured board, roll to $^1/_8$-inch thick. Cut with a pastry wheel or knife into strips about 3 inches long and $^1/_2$-inch wide. Place about 1 inch apart on ungreased baking sheets and bake, uncovered, at 400° for 10–12 minutes, or until lightly browned and crisp. Makes 6–7 dozen.

Cheese Crispies

$^1/_2$ c soft butter
1 c finely grated cheddar
   cheese

1 c flour
Pinch of cayenne
1 c crisp rice cereal

Cream butter and cheese together in medium bowl. Stir in flour, cayenne, and cereal. Mix well. Shape into 1-inch balls. Place on ungreased baking sheets. Flatten with fork. Bake at 375° for 10–15 minutes until golden. They will be more crispy if they are pressed thin. Makes approximately 3 dozen.

Chocolate-Peppermint Pretzels

1 c powdered sugar
$\frac{1}{2}$ c butter, softened
$\frac{1}{2}$ c shortening
1 egg
$1\frac{1}{2}$ tsp vanilla

$2\frac{1}{2}$ c flour
$\frac{1}{2}$ c cocoa
1 tsp salt
$\frac{1}{4}$ c crushed candy canes

CHOCOLATE COATING:

2 squares unsweetened chocolate
2 tbsp butter

2 c powdered sugar
3–4 tbsp water

FOR COATING:

Melt chocolate and butter; remove from heat. Beat in sugar and water until smooth.

FOR PRETZELS:

Mix sugar, butter, shortening, egg, and vanilla. Stir in dry ingredients, except candy canes. Knead level tablespoons of dough by hand until it's the right consistency for molding. Roll into pencil-like ropes, about 9 inches long. Twist into pretzel shapes on ungreased baking sheet. Bake in 375° oven until set, about 9 minutes. Let stand 1–2 minutes before removing from baking sheet; cool completely. Dip tops of pretzels into coating and sprinkle with crushed candy canes.

Coconutty Banana Bites

5 firm bananas
2 tbsp lemon juice

1 c vanilla yogurt
2 c flaked coconut,
    toasted

(To toast coconut, bake at 350° for 10 minutes or until light golden brown.)

Cut bananas into bite-sized pieces. Dip into lemon juice and drain off excess. Dip into yogurt, then roll gently in coconut to coat. Serve immediately or refrigerate up to 2 hours before serving. Serve with cocktail toothpicks. Makes approximately 30.

Stuffed Dates

1 pkg dates
1 pkg cheddar cheese

1 pkg bacon

Cut bacon strips in half. Fry bacon until halfway cooked. Drain. Cut cheese into small lengths, to taste. Slit dates and stuff with 1 length of cheese each. Wrap with ½ slice bacon. Broil until the bacon is cooked.

Jell-O Trees

2 (8-serving size) pkgs lime Jell-O powder	1 pkg unflavored gelatin
	3 c boiling water

Mix gelatin in ¼ cup cold water and let sit for 1 minute. Add Jell-O powder to boiled water; add gelatin mixture and mix until completely dissolved. Spray a baking sheet or large cake pan with cooking spray to prevent sticking. When mixture has cooled to room temperature, pour into pan and refrigerate until firm, at least 3 hours. Using Christmas tree-shaped cookie cutters, cut into shapes.

Easy Onion Chip Dip

1 pkg onion soup mix	1 container sour cream

Mix well; serve with plain or rippled chips.

*Worship the LORD
your God,
and his blessing will be
on your food and water.*

EXODUS 23:25

Christmas
SWEETS

"Then the King will say TO THOSE ON HIS RIGHT, 'COME, YOU WHO ARE BLESSED BY MY FATHER; TAKE YOUR INHERITANCE, THE KINGDOM PREPARED FOR YOU SINCE THE CREATION OF THE WORLD. FOR I WAS HUNGRY AND YOU GAVE ME SOMETHING TO EAT. . . .' THE KING WILL REPLY, 'I TELL YOU THE TRUTH, WHATEVER YOU DID FOR ONE OF THE LEAST OF THESE BROTHERS OF MINE, YOU DID FOR ME.' "

MATTHEW 25:34–35, 40

Bars and Squares

"He has shown kindness

BY GIVING YOU RAIN

FROM HEAVEN AND CROPS IN THEIR SEASONS;

HE PROVIDES YOU WITH PLENTY OF FOOD

AND FILLS YOUR HEARTS WITH JOY."

ACTS 14:17

Reese's Squares

2 sticks butter, melted
5 c confectioners' sugar
1 c semisweet chocolate chips

2 ½ c peanut butter
4 tbsp butter, melted

Mix 2 sticks melted butter and peanut butter until smooth. Add confectioners' sugar. Put into a 9x13-inch baking pan. Pat down firmly. Combine 4 tbsp melted butter and chocolate chips until smooth. Spread on top of peanut butter mixture. Refrigerate 2 hours. Cut into squares.

Chocolate Cherry Bars

1 pkg fudge cake mix
1 tsp almond extract

1 large can cherry pie filling
2 eggs, beaten

Combine all ingredients in a large bowl until well mixed. Spray 9x13-inch pan with cooking spray. Pour batter into pan and bake at 350° for 25–30 minutes. When cool, add frosting. Can also be served with whipped topping or ice cream.

FUDGE FROSTING:

1 c sugar
5 tbsp butter or margarine

$\frac{1}{3}$ c milk
1 c chocolate chips

Combine sugar, butter, and milk in saucepan. Boil 1 minute, stirring constantly. Remove from heat and stir in chips until smooth. Let thicken slightly and pour over cooled bars.

Double-Chocolate Mud Bars

½ c butter, softened
1 c sugar
2 large eggs, separated
1½ c flour
1 tsp baking powder
½ tsp salt

1 c walnuts, chopped
½ c semisweet chocolate chips
1 c miniature marshmallows
1 c brown sugar, firmly packed
1 c M&Ms (optional)

Beat together butter and sugar. Add egg yolks one at a time. In a different bowl, mix together flour, baking powder, and salt. Fold flour mixture into butter mixture. Press mixture into greased 9x13-inch baking pan. Pack down firmly. Sprinkle walnuts, chocolate chips, marshmallows, and M&Ms over top of mixture in pan.

Beat egg whites at high speed until stiff peaks form. Fold in brown sugar. Spread over mixture in pan. Bake 35 minutes at 350°. Cool completely; cut into squares.

Chocolate Cappuccino Brownies

BROWNIE LAYER:

4 oz fine-quality bittersweet chocolate (not unsweetened), chopped

3/4 stick (6 tbsp) unsalted butter, cut into pieces

1 tbsp instant espresso powder, dissolved in 1/2 tbsp boiling water

3/4 c sugar

1 tsp vanilla extract

2 large eggs

1/2 c all-purpose flour

1/4 tsp salt

1/2 c walnuts, chopped

CREAM CHEESE FROSTING:

4 oz cream cheese, softened

3 tbsp unsalted butter, softened

3/4 c confectioners' sugar, sifted

1/2 tsp vanilla extract

1/2 tsp cinnamon

GLAZE:

3 oz fine-quality bittersweet chocolate (not unsweetened)

1 tbsp unsalted butter

1/4 c heavy cream

2 1/4 tsp instant espresso powder, dissolved in 1/2 tbsp boiling water

Preheat oven to 350° and butter and flour an 8-inch square baking pan, tapping out excess flour.

BROWNIE LAYER:

In a heavy 1½-quart saucepan, melt chocolate and butter with espresso mixture over low heat, stirring until smooth, and remove pan from heat. Cool mixture to lukewarm and whisk in sugar and vanilla. Add eggs, one at a time, whisking well until mixture is glossy and smooth. Stir in flour and salt until just combined and stir in walnuts.

Spread batter evenly in pan and bake in middle of oven 22–25 minutes, or until a tester comes out with crumbs adhering to it. Cool brownie layer completely in pan on a rack.

CREAM CHEESE FROSTING:

In a bowl with an electric mixer, beat cream cheese and butter until light and fluffy. Add confectioners' sugar, vanilla, and cinnamon, and beat until combined well. Spread frosting evenly over brownie layer. Chill brownies 1 hour, or until frosting is firm.

GLAZE:

In a double boiler or metal bowl set over a saucepan of barely simmering water, melt chocolate and butter with cream and espresso mixture, stirring until smooth, and remove top of double boiler or bowl from heat. Cool glaze to room temperature.

Spread glaze carefully over frosting. Chill brownies, covered, until cold, at least 3 hours.

Cut chilled brownies into 24 squares and remove them from pan while still cold. Serve brownies cold or at room temperature. Brownies keep, covered and chilled, in one layer, 5 days.

Caramel Cashew Bars

8 Rhodes Texas rolls,
   thawed and raised
1½ c chocolate chips
14 oz caramels, unwrapped
⅓ c evaporated milk

⅓ c butter
1⅔ c powdered sugar
2 c cashew halves
½ c semisweet chocolate
   chips

Press 4 rolls together and roll into a 9x13-inch rectangle. Place in a 9x13-inch pan sprayed with nonstick cooking spray. Sprinkle with 1½ cups chocolate chips. Repeat with remaining rolls and place over top of chocolate chips. Bake at 350° for 15 minutes. Let cool.

Place caramels, milk, and butter in medium saucepan. Melt on low heat, stirring occasionally until smooth. Remove from heat. Add powdered sugar and stir until smooth. Fold in cashews. Pour mixture over baked crust. Melt ½ cup chocolate chips in microwave and drizzle over caramel layer. Refrigerate until firm.

Cinnamon Toffee Bars

½ c butter
2 c brown sugar, packed
2 eggs, beaten
2 tsp vanilla extract
2 c all-purpose flour

2 tsp baking powder
¼ tsp salt
1 tsp ground cinnamon
1 c pecans, chopped
12 oz semisweet chocolate chips

Cook butter and brown sugar over low heat, in a saucepan, until mixture comes to a boil. Remove from heat and let cool.

Preheat oven to 350°. Grease a 12x18-inch jelly roll pan.

In a medium bowl, stir together butter mixture, eggs, and vanilla. Sift together flour, baking powder, salt, and cinnamon; stir into egg mixture until well blended. Then stir in pecans. Spread batter onto prepared jelly roll pan. Bake in preheated oven for 25 minutes. Remove from oven and immediately sprinkle chocolate chips over whole sheet. Let stand for 5 minutes, then spread chocolate evenly over entire surface. Cut into squares.

Candy Bar Squares

³/₄ c butter or margarine,
softened
¹/₄ c peanut butter
1 c brown sugar, packed
1 tsp baking soda
2 c quick oats
1¹/₂ c flour

1 egg
1 14-oz can sweetened
condensed milk (not
evaporated)
4 c candy bars,
chopped (like Snickers
or Milky Way)

Preheat oven to 350°. In large bowl, combine butter and peanut butter. Add brown sugar and baking soda; beat well. Stir in oats and flour. Reserve 1¾ cups crumb mixture.

Stir egg into remaining crumb mixture; press firmly on bottom of ungreased 15x10x1-inch baking pan. Bake 15 minutes.

Spread sweetened condensed milk over baked crust. Stir together remaining crumb mixture and candy bar pieces; sprinkle evenly over top. Bake 25 minutes or until golden. Cool. Cut into bars. Store covered at room temperature.

Butterscotch Bars

1 12-oz pkg butterscotch
    morsels
½ c butter or margarine
2 c graham cracker crumbs
1 c walnuts, finely chopped
1 8-oz pkg cream cheese,
    softened

1 14-oz can sweetened
    condensed milk (not
    evaporated)
1 egg
1 tsp vanilla extract

Preheat oven to 350°. Grease a 9x13-inch baking dish; set aside. In medium saucepan, melt morsels and butter over low heat, stirring often. Stir in crumbs and nuts. Press half of mixture into bottom of pan.

In large mixing bowl, with electric mixer on medium, beat cream cheese until fluffy. Beat in condensed milk, egg, and vanilla until smooth. Pour over crumb mixture in pan. Sprinkle remaining crumb mixture on top. Bake 25–30 minutes or until toothpick inserted in center comes out clean. Cool completely on wire rack. Refrigerate.

Coconut Bars

2 sticks margarine, melted
1 c sugar
1 egg, slightly beaten
½ c milk

1 c nuts, chopped
1 can coconut
1 c graham cracker crumbs
Whole graham crackers

Combine first 4 ingredients in a saucepan and bring to a boil; cook one minute, then add nuts, coconut, and cracker crumbs. Grease 9x13x2-inch pan. Line with whole graham crackers. Pour above mixture over whole graham crackers, then add another layer of whole graham crackers. Spread with icing.

ICING:

¾ stick margarine
2 c confectioners' sugar

1 tbsp vanilla extract
1 tbsp milk

Mix all ingredients together. Spread on top of graham crackers. Refrigerate for several hours to allow graham crackers to soften slightly. Cut into strips or squares.

Caramel Apple Bars

BASE:

2 c flour

2 c quick rolled oats

1½ c brown sugar, firmly packed

1 tsp baking soda

1¼ c butter, melted

FILLING:

½ c flour

20 oz (1½ c) caramel ice cream
   topping

2 c Golden Delicious apples,
   chopped and peeled

½ c walnuts, chopped

Heat oven to 350°. Grease 15x10x1-inch baking pan. In large bowl, mix base ingredients until crumbly. Press half of base mixture into bottom of greased pan. Bake 8–10 minutes. In a small pan, mix flour and caramel; bring to a boil over medium heat, 3–5 minutes or until mixture thickens, stirring constantly. Remove base from oven; sprinkle apples and walnuts over base. Pour caramel mixture over apples and walnuts. Sprinkle remaining base mix on and bake for 20–25 minutes or until golden brown. Cool; refrigerate for 30 minutes or until set. Cut into bars. Can also be served warm.

Speedy Brownies

2 c sugar
1³/₄ c flour
½ c baking cocoa
1 tsp salt

5 eggs
1 c vegetable oil
1 tsp vanilla extract
1 c semisweet chocolate
 chips

In a mixing bowl, combine first 7 ingredients; beat until smooth. Pour into a greased 9x13-inch baking pan. Sprinkle with chocolate chips. Bake at 350° for 30 minutes, or until a toothpick inserted near center comes out clean. Cool in pan on a wire rack.

Orange-Date Bars

1 c dates, chopped
⅓ c sugar
⅓ c vegetable oil
½ c orange juice
1 c flour

½ c pecans, chopped
1 egg
1½ tsp baking powder
1 tbsp orange peel,
 grated

Combine dates, sugar, oil, and juice in a saucepan. Cook 5 minutes to soften dates. Cool. Add remaining ingredients. Spread into a greased 8x8-inch pan. Bake at 350° for 25 minutes. Cool before cutting.

Peanut Butter Oatmeal Bars

½ c butter
½ c sugar
½ c brown sugar
1 egg
½ c peanut butter

½ tsp baking soda
¼ tsp salt
½ tsp vanilla extract
1 c flour
1 c oatmeal

TOPPING #1
1 c semisweet chocolate chips

TOPPING #2
½ c confectioners' sugar, sifted
¼ c peanut butter
2–4 tbsp cream or milk

Cream butter and sugars. Blend in egg, peanut butter, baking soda, salt, and vanilla. Stir in flour and oatmeal. Spread in 9x13-inch pan and bake at 350° for 20–25 minutes. (See toppings.) Remove from oven and immediately sprinkle with chocolate chips. Let stand 5 minutes; spread over top. Combine confectioners' sugar, peanut butter, and milk; drizzle over chocolate layer. Cool; cut into bars.

White Chocolate Squares

1 12-oz pkg white chocolate
   chips, divided
$\frac{1}{4}$ c butter or margarine
2 c flour
$\frac{1}{2}$ tsp baking powder
1 tsp vanilla extract

1 14-oz can sweetened
   condensed milk (not
   evaporated)
1 c pecans or walnuts,
   chopped
1 large egg
Confectioners' sugar

Preheat oven to 350°. Grease a 9x13-inch baking pan. In large sauce-pan over low heat, melt 1 cup chips and butter. Stir in flour and baking powder until blended. Stir in vanilla, sweetened condensed milk, nuts, egg, and remaining chips. Spoon mixture into prepared pan.

   Bake 20–25 minutes. Cool. Sprinkle with confectioners' sugar; cut into squares. Store covered at room temperature.

Caramel Pecan Brownies

24 vanilla caramels
4 tbsp milk
4 eggs
1½ c sugar
½ stick butter, melted
1 tsp vanilla extract

1½ c flour
1 tsp baking powder
1 c pecans, chopped
1 tsp salt
Confectioners' sugar

Stir together caramels and milk over medium heat until caramels are melted. Set aside. In mixing bowl, beat eggs; gradually beat in sugar. Blend in butter, caramel mixture, and vanilla. Stir together flour, baking powder, and salt; add to caramel mixture. Fold in pecans. Pour into greased baking pan. Bake at 350° for 30–40 minutes. Sift confectioners' sugar on top. Cut into bars.

Chewy Bars

1 box yellow cake mix
1 c light brown sugar, packed
2¾ c oil
4 eggs

1½ c milk
¼ c cinnamon
2 c nuts (optional)

Mix all dry ingredients. Blend eggs and milk together, beating slightly. Add to dry mix alternately with oil. Add nuts. Spread into an ungreased sheet pan. Bake at 350° for 20–25 minutes. Let cool for 30 minutes before cutting into squares.

Chocolate Peanut Bars

1 pkg (18¼ oz) white cake mix
1 c peanut butter, divided
1 egg
1 pkg (8 oz) cream cheese,
    softened
⅓ c milk
¼ c sugar
1 c (6 oz) semisweet
    chocolate chips
¾ c salted peanuts

In a mixing bowl, beat cake mix, ⅔ cup peanut butter, and egg until crumbly. Press into a greased 9x13-inch baking pan. In a mixing bowl, combine cream cheese and remaining peanut butter. Gradually beat in milk and sugar. Carefully spread over crust. Sprinkle with chocolate chips and peanuts.

    Bake at 350° for 25–30 minutes or until edges are lightly browned and center is set. Cool completely before cutting. Store in refrigerator.

Caramel Brownies

2 c sugar
³/₄ c baking cocoa
1 c vegetable oil
4 eggs
¹/₄ c milk
1¹/₂ c all-purpose flour
1 tsp salt
1 tsp baking powder

1 c (6 oz) semisweet
    chocolate chips
1 c chopped walnuts,
    divided
1 pkg (14 oz) caramels
1 can (14 oz)
    sweetened
    condensed milk
    (not evaporated)

In a mixing bowl, combine sugar, cocoa, oil, eggs, and milk. In a different bowl, combine flour, salt, and baking powder; add to egg mixture and mix until combined. Fold in chocolate chips and ¹/₂ cup walnuts. Spoon ²/₃ of batter into a greased 9x13-inch baking pan. Bake at 350° for 12 minutes.

Meanwhile, in a saucepan, heat caramels and sweetened condensed milk over low heat until caramels are melted. Pour over baked brownie layer. Sprinkle with remaining walnuts. Drop remaining batter by teaspoonfuls over caramel layer; carefully swirl brownie batter with a knife. Bake 35–40 minutes longer or until toothpick inserted near center comes out with moist crumbs. Cool.

Seven-Layer Bars

½ c butter
1 c graham cracker crumbs
1 c flaked coconut
6 oz butterscotch chips

6 oz chocolate chips
1 c nuts, chopped
1 can sweetened condensed
    milk (not evaporated)

Preheat oven to 325°. Melt butter in a 9x13-inch pan. Add next 5 ingredients in layers and carefully pour sweetened condensed milk on top. Bake for 25–30 minutes or until slightly brown.

Blueberry Cheese Squares

1 roll prepared cookie dough
    (lemon, butterscotch, or
    other flavor)
1 8-oz pkg cream cheese,
    softened

1 c sour cream
¼ c sugar
1 egg
½ tsp vanilla extract
1 can blueberry pie filling

Preheat oven to 375°. Slice dough in ¼-inch slices. Overlap in ungreased 9x13-inch pan. Bake for 12–15 minutes, then allow to cool a few minutes. Meanwhile, combine cream cheese, sour cream, sugar, egg, and vanilla. Beat until smooth. Pour pie filling over cookie crust. Top with cream mixture and bake for 25–30 minutes. Serves 12.

Chocolate Syrup Brownies

½ c butter or margarine,
  softened
1 c sugar
1 16-oz can (1½ c) chocolate-
  flavored syrup

4 eggs
1¼ c flour
1 c walnuts, chopped
Quick Frosting

Cream butter and sugar; beat in eggs. Blend in syrup and flour; stir in nuts. Pour into greased 9x13-inch pan. Bake at 350° for 30–35 minutes. Cool slightly; top with Quick Frosting.

QUICK FROSTING:

⅔ c sugar
3 tbsp milk

3 tbsp butter
½ c chocolate chips

In a saucepan, mix first 3 ingredients, then bring to a boil; boil for 30 seconds. Remove from heat; stir in chocolate chips until melted. Will be thin. Spread over brownies. Cool; cut into bars.

Rhubarb Bars

3 c cut rhubarb
1½ c sugar
1 tsp vanilla extract
2 tbsp cornstarch
¼ c water
1½ c oatmeal

1 c brown sugar
1 c shortening (part margarine)
½ c walnuts, chopped
1½ c flour
½ tsp baking soda

Cook first 5 ingredients until thick. In a separate bowl, mix remaining ingredients; pat ¾ mixture into a 9x13-inch pan. Pour and spread cooked rhubarb mixture over crust. Sprinkle remaining crumbs on top. Bake at 375° for 30–35 minutes.

Chocolate Caramel Bars

2 c flour
1 c brown sugar
½ c butter
1 c pecans, finely chopped

⅔ c butter
½ c brown sugar
1 c butterscotch chips
1 c semisweet chocolate
    chips

Mix flour, 1 cup brown sugar, ½ cup butter in a food processor or with a pastry blender. Pat this crust into bottom of a 9x13-inch pan. Sprinkle pecans on top of crust. Melt ⅔ cup butter and ½ cup brown sugar and cook until bubbly (about 2–3 minutes), then pour mixture over top of crust. Bake at 350° for 15–20 minutes, until melted butter and sugar are bubbling on top and crust is lightly browned. Remove from oven and sprinkle a mixture of butterscotch chips and semisweet chocolate chips over top. Let chips melt and then swirl them together over top of crust. Cut while still warm into 48 squares.

Frosted Peanut Butter Bars

½ c peanut butter
⅓ c shortening
1½ c brown sugar, packed
2 eggs
1 tsp vanilla extract

1½ c all-purpose flour
1½ tsp baking powder
½ tsp salt
¼ c milk

FROSTING:

⅔ c creamy peanut butter
½ c shortening

4 c confectioners' sugar
⅓ to ½ c milk

TOPPING:

½ c semisweet chocolate chips   1 tsp shortening

In a mixing bowl, cream peanut butter, shortening, and brown sugar. Beat in eggs and vanilla. Combine flour, baking powder, and salt; gradually add to creamed mixture. Add milk; mix well. Transfer to a greased 15x10x1-inch baking pan. Bake at 350° for 16–20 minutes or until a toothpick inserted near center comes out clean. Cool.

For frosting, in a mixing bowl, cream peanut butter, shortening, and confectioners' sugar. Gradually beat in enough milk to achieve spreading consistency. Frost bars. Melt chocolate chips and shortening; stir until smooth. Drizzle over frosting. Refrigerate.

Cakes

But if we have

FOOD AND CLOTHING,

WE WILL BE CONTENT WITH THAT.

1 TIMOTHY 6:8

Almond Lemon Cake

8 egg whites
1 dash cream of tartar
1 c sugar, divided
2 c flour
1 tsp baking powder
⅛ tsp salt
1 c butter or margarine, softened

1½ tbsp lemon peel, grated
1 tbsp lemon juice
1 c sour cream
2 tsp vanilla extract
1 c blanched almonds,
    finely chopped

In a bowl, beat egg whites with cream of tartar until stiff. Gradually beat in ½ cup sugar. In another bowl, stir together flour, baking powder, and salt.

In a large bowl, cream butter or margarine with remaining ½ cup sugar. Beat in lemon peel, lemon juice, sour cream, and vanilla. Stir flour mixture into butter mixture, along with about ⅓ of beaten egg whites. Fold in rest of egg whites gently but thoroughly. Stir in almonds. Turn batter into greased and floured tube pan. Bake at 350° for about 70 minutes, or until it tests done with a toothpick. Cool on a wire rack.

Almond Pound Cake

1 c butter, softened	8 oz almond paste
2 c white sugar	1 c confectioners' sugar
6 eggs, room temperature	4 tbsp milk
1¾ c all-purpose flour	½ c blanched almonds
½ tsp salt	4 drops red food coloring
2 tsp almond extract	4 drops green food coloring

Preheat oven to 325°. Grease and flour a 10-inch Bundt pan. In a large bowl, cream butter and sugar together until well mixed with an electric mixer. Add eggs, one at a time, and beat until mixture is light and fluffy. Blend in flour and salt. Mix in almond extract. Turn batter into prepared pan. Bake for 60 minutes, or until a toothpick inserted in center of cake comes out clean. Cool in pan for 10 minutes. Remove from pan and transfer to a wire rack to continue cooling.

Break off tablespoon-sized pieces of almond paste, and shape into holly leaves. Using the tip of a knife, score shaped holly leaves to resemble veins in leaves. Mix green food coloring with a small amount of water and brush holly leaves, repeating until desired color is reached. Set aside on waxed paper. Break off 2 tablespoons of almond paste, and knead in several drops of red food coloring. When color of almond paste is a bright red, break off smaller pieces. Roll into balls to resemble holly berries. Place on waxed paper. In a small bowl, combine 1 cup confectioners' sugar and milk. Mix until smooth. When cake has cooled, drizzle with confectioners' sugar glaze. Top with blanched almonds, and garnish with marzipan holly leaves and berries.

Chocolate Caramel Cake

1²/₃ c flour
1¹/₂ c sugar
²/₃ c cocoa powder
1¹/₂ tsp baking powder
1 tsp salt
1¹/₂ c buttermilk

¹/₂ c shortening
2 eggs
1¹/₂ tsp vanilla extract
30 caramels
1 can sweetened condensed
  milk (not evaporated)

Beat first 9 ingredients in large mixing bowl on low speed, scraping sides of bowl, until blended. Beat on high, scraping sides occasionally for an additional 3 minutes. Pour half the mixture into a greased and floured 9x13-inch pan, and bake at 350° for 15 minutes. In the meantime, melt caramels and sweetened condensed milk together. Spread over warm cake. Put remaining cake mixture on top of caramel mixture. Bake an additional 15 minutes, or until done. May be served warm with vanilla ice cream for a tasty treat.

Snicker Doodle Cake

1 German chocolate cake mix
1 14-oz pkg caramels
1 stick margarine
¹/₃ c milk
³/₄ c chocolate chips
1 c walnuts, chopped

Prepare cake mix, following package directions. Pour half the batter into a greased 9x13-inch pan. Bake at 350° for 20 minutes. Melt caramels with margarine and milk in saucepan over low heat, stirring frequently. Pour over baked cake. Sprinkle with chocolate chips and nuts. Spoon remaining cake batter over caramel layer. Bake at 250° for 20 minutes. Increase temperature to 350° and bake an additional 10 minutes.

Angel Cake Surprise

1 10-inch tube pan angel
   food cake or pound cake
1 3-oz pkg strawberry-
   flavored gelatin
1 15-oz can sliced peaches
3 bananas

1 20-oz can crushed
   pineapple, drained
   (optional)
1 5-oz pkg instant
   vanilla pudding mix
1 8-oz container frozen
   whipped topping,
   thawed

Break angel food or pound cake into bite-sized pieces. Put
into a 9x13-inch pan (preferably glass). Dissolve 1 package of
flavored gelatin in 1 cup of hot water and pour over cake
pieces, spreading to the edges of pan. Drain peaches and
pour juice over gelatin in pan. Slice bananas on top of gelatin. Arrange peach slices on top of banana slices. If desired,
add crushed pineapple. Prepare instant pudding according to
instructions on box and spread evenly over fruit. Spread
whipped topping on top of pudding. Try to keep layers separate. Refrigerate at least 2 hours before serving.

Apple Bundt Cake

2 c apples: peeled, cored,
    and diced
1 tbsp sugar
1 tsp ground cinnamon
3 c flour
3 tsp baking powder
½ tsp salt

2 c sugar
1 c vegetable oil
¼ c orange juice
2½ tsp vanilla extract
4 eggs
1 c walnuts, chopped
¼ c confectioners' sugar

Preheat oven to 350°. Grease and flour a 10-inch Bundt or tube pan. In a medium bowl, combine diced apples, 1 tablespoon sugar, and 1 teaspoon cinnamon; set aside. Sift together flour, baking powder, and salt; set aside. In a large bowl, combine 2 cups sugar, oil, orange juice, vanilla, and eggs. Beat at high speed until smooth. Stir in flour mixture. Fold in chopped walnuts. Pour ⅓ of the batter into prepared pan. Sprinkle with ½ of the apple mixture. Alternate layers of batter and filling, ending with batter. Bake for 55–60 minutes, or until top springs back when lightly touched. Let cool in pan for 10 minutes, then turn out onto a wire rack and cool completely. Sprinkle with confectioners' sugar.

Apple Sheet Cake

PASTRY:

3 c flour
1½ tsp baking powder
1 tsp salt

½ c shortening
1 c cold milk

APPLE FILLING:

3 lbs apples: peeled, cored,
and sliced
1 c sugar

1 tsp ground cinnamon
2 tbsp flour
½ c butter

FROSTING:

2½ c confectioners' sugar
3 tbsp milk

⅓ c butter, softened
½ tsp vanilla extract

Preheat oven to 400°. In a large bowl, combine 3 cups flour, baking powder, and salt. Cut in shortening to consistency of coarse crumbs. Stir in milk slowly until completely blended. Separate dough into two balls. Roll out one ball of dough to fit a 15x10-inch pan with some dough extending over edge of pan.

In a large bowl, combine sliced apples, sugar, cinnamon, and 2 tablespoons flour. Place filling in an even layer over prepared crust. Thinly slice ½ cup butter and evenly distribute over apples. Roll out remaining dough and place over apple filling. Seal edges and prick top all over with a fork. Bake in preheated oven for 30 minutes. Cool 5 minutes before frosting.

TO MAKE FROSTING:

Combine ingredients in a bowl; beat until smooth and creamy.

Butter Cookie Almond Wreath Cake

1 c unsalted butter, room
    temperature
1 c almond paste, room
    temperature

1 c confectioners' sugar
1 tsp almond extract
2 egg yolks
$\frac{1}{2}$ tsp salt
$2\frac{1}{2}$ c flour

In a large mixing bowl, cream together butter, almond paste, and sugar until very smooth. Blend in almond extract and egg yolks. In a separate bowl, stir together salt and flour, then blend into butter mixture. Chill dough for 30 minutes. Preheat oven to 350°. Cover several cookie sheets with parchment paper. Cut off portions of dough and shape into ropes about the thickness of your thumb, each 1 inch longer than the previous, beginning at 4 inches and ending at 18 inches. You will have 15 strands. Shape each strand into a circle and place on parchment-covered baking sheets. Bake for 10 minutes or until pale gold. Cool.

ROYAL ICING:

1 lb (3–4 c) confectioners' sugar

1–2 egg whites

1 tsp almond extract

Place powdered sugar in large bowl. Add one egg white and almond extract. Mix with electric beater until smooth and well blended. If necessary, add part or all of the second egg white. The icing needs to be thin enough to press through the fine tip of a pastry bag. (In place of a pastry bag, you can use a cone made from waxed paper. Snip off bottom of cone to form a fine-tip opening.) Spoon icing into pastry bag (or waxed paper cone).

TO ASSEMBLE CAKE:

Place largest cookie ring on a serving plate. Press Royal Icing through pastry bag in a zigzag pattern all the way around the ring. Top with next largest ring. Repeat zigzag piping procedure. Continue stacking and frosting rings to form a balanced tower. Decorate the top with a fresh rose and the sides with flags, flowers, marzipan candies, or cracker bonbons, using Royal Icing to adhere them to the cake. To serve cake, lift top part of the tower off, and break remaining rings into 2- or 3-inch pieces.

Snowball Cake

2 envelopes unflavored gelatin	1 8-oz can crushed
4 tbsp cold water	pineapple, drained
1 c boiling water	2 large containers
1 c sugar	Cool Whip
2 tbsp lemon juice	1 angel food cake
	1 small can coconut

Mix gelatin with cold water. Add boiling water, sugar, lemon juice, and pineapple. Set in refrigerator to thicken for 30 minutes. Fold in 1 container of Cool Whip. Set aside. Crumble half of cake in 9x13-inch pan (bite-size pieces). Spoon half of mixture over cake. Repeat with other half. Frost with 1 container of Cool Whip. Sprinkle with coconut.

Molasses Cake

1 tsp baking powder	2 c flour
1 tsp baking soda	1 c molasses
1 tsp cinnamon	1 egg
1 tsp nutmeg	½ c butter
¾ c sugar	1 c sour cream

Mix all dry ingredients together. Add molasses, egg, butter, and sour cream together. Mix well. Bake at 350° for 30–35 minutes. Bakes a 9x13-inch, 2-layer cake.

Black Forest Cake

2 20-oz cans tart pitted
   cherries, undrained
1 c sugar
¼ c cornstarch
1½ tsp vanilla extract

2 9-inch chocolate
   cake layers,
   baked and cooled
3 c cold whipping
   cream
⅓ c confectioners'
   sugar

Drain cherries, reserving ½ cup juice. Combine reserved cherry juices, cherries, sugar, and cornstarch in saucepan. Cook and stir over low heat until thickened. Add vanilla; stir. Divide each cake layer in half horizontally. Crumble one half layer; set aside. Beat cold whipping cream and confectioners' sugar in a large bowl with an electric mixer on high until stiff peaks form. Reserve 1½ cups whipped cream for decorative piping.

Place one cake layer on a serving plate. Spread with 1 cup whipped cream; top with ¾ cup cherry topping. Top with second cake layer, 1 cup whipped cream, and ¾ cup cherry topping; top with third cake layer. Frost cake sides with remaining whipped cream; pat gently with reserved cake crumbs.

Spoon reserved 1½ cups whipped cream into pastry bag fitted with star tip; pipe around top and bottom edges of cake. Spoon remaining topping over top of cake.

Red Velvet Cake

½ c shortening
1½ c sugar
2 eggs
2 tbsp cocoa
1½ oz red food coloring
1 tsp salt

2½ c flour
1 tsp vanilla extract
1 c buttermilk
1 tsp baking soda
1 tbsp vinegar

Cream shortening; add sugar gradually. Add eggs, one at a time; beat well. Make paste of cocoa and coloring; add to creamed mixture. Add salt, flour, and vanilla alternately with buttermilk, beating well after each addition. Sprinkle soda over vinegar; pour vinegar over batter. Stir until thoroughly mixed. Bake in three 8-inch square pans or two 9-inch square pans for 30 minutes at 350°.

CREAM CHEESE FROSTING:

2 3-oz pkgs cream cheese,
    softened
6 tbsp butter, softened

1 tsp vanilla extract
2 c confectioners' sugar, sifted

Blend all ingredients until smooth.

Candy

"Do not work for

FOOD THAT SPOILS,

BUT FOR FOOD THAT

ENDURES TO ETERNAL LIFE,

WHICH THE SON OF MAN WILL GIVE YOU.

ON HIM GOD THE FATHER

HAS PLACED HIS SEAL OF APPROVAL."

JOHN 6:27

Soft Peanut Butter Peanut Brittle

A softer alternative to a traditional holiday favorite

2 c sugar
¼ c water
1½ c light corn syrup
2 c salted peanuts

2–2½ c peanut butter
½ tsp vanilla extract
1½ tsp baking soda

Combine sugar and water in heavy saucepan. Bring mixture to full rolling boil over high heat, stirring constantly. Stir in corn syrup. Cook to hard-crack stage, 300°. Meanwhile, mix peanuts, peanut butter, and vanilla. Remove syrup from heat; at once add peanut butter mixture and baking soda; stir. Working quickly, pour onto buttered cookie sheet; spread with fork. Cool; break into pieces.

Fantastic Fudge

²⁄₃ c evaporated milk   1½ c miniature marshmallows
1²⁄₃ c sugar   ½ tsp salt
1½ c chocolate chips   1 tsp vanilla extract

Combine milk and sugar; bring to a boil for 5 minutes. Add chocolate chips and marshmallows. Stir until blended. Add salt and vanilla and pour into a buttered 8-inch square baking dish to cool.

Flavor variations:

MOCHA: Dissolve 2 teaspoons instant coffee granules in 1 teaspoon hot water. Add with chocolate.

MINT: Add ¾ cup mint chips, ¾ cup chocolate chips.

MARBLE: Make fudge with white chocolate and drizzle in melted chocolate chips.

CHOCOLATE ORANGE: Add 2 teaspoons freshly grated orange peel.

PEANUT BUTTER: Substitute peanut butter chips for chocolate chips.

WHITE ALMOND: Substitute white chocolate chips and ½ cup slivered almonds.

MAPLE: Substitute butterscotch chips and add maple flavoring to taste.

Sticks and Stones Candy Bark

1 11-oz pkg butterscotch
   morsels, divided
1½ c semisweet chocolate
   morsels
½ c creamy peanut butter

2 c dry-roasted peanuts
1 10-oz pkg semisweet
   chocolate-covered raisins
2 c thin pretzel sticks

Butter a 9x13-inch glass baking dish. Microwave 1⅓ cups butterscotch morsels, semisweet morsels, and peanut butter in large,
microwave-safe bowl on high for 1 minute; stir. Microwave at additional 10- to 20-second intervals, stirring until smooth. Add pretzels,
peanuts, and chocolate-covered raisins; stir well to coat. Spread into
prepared baking dish. Place remaining butterscotch morsels in small,
heavy-duty plastic bag. Microwave on medium-high (70 percent)
power for 30 seconds; knead bag to mix. Microwave at additional
10- to 20-second intervals, kneading until smooth. Cut tiny corner
from bag; squeeze to drizzle over candy. Refrigerate for 1 hour or
until firm. Break into bite-sized pieces.

Festive Holiday Bark

16 oz vanilla-flavored
    confectioners' coating
2 c small pretzel twists

$\frac{1}{2}$ c red and green
    candy-coated
    chocolate

Line a cookie sheet with waxed paper or parchment paper. Place confectioners' coating in a microwave-safe bowl. Microwave for $2\frac{1}{2}$ minutes. Stir; microwave at 30-second intervals until completely melted and smooth. Place pretzels and candy-coated chocolate pieces in a large bowl. Pour melted coating over and stir until well coated. Spread onto waxed paper-lined baking sheet. Let stand until firm or place in refrigerator to set up faster. Store in a container at room temperature.

Microwave Dump Fudge

1 lb confectioners' sugar, sifted
1 stick real butter, sliced
$\frac{1}{2}$ c cocoa

$\frac{1}{4}$ c milk
$1\frac{1}{2}$ tsp vanilla extract
$\frac{1}{2}$ c nuts, chopped
    (if desired)

Dump confectioners' sugar, butter slices, cocoa, and milk into microwave-safe bowl. Microwave on high for 2 minutes. Remove; stir vigorously to blend. Add vanilla and nuts. Pour into an 8-inch square pan lined with foil and buttered. Refrigerate until firm.

Milk Chocolate Popcorn

12 c popcorn, popped
2½ c salted peanuts
1 c light corn syrup

1 11½-oz pkg milk
  chocolate morsels
¼ c butter or margarine

Preheat oven to 300°. Grease a large roasting pan. Line a large bowl or serving plate with waxed paper. Combine popcorn and nuts in prepared roasting pan. Combine corn syrup, morsels, and butter in medium, heavy-duty saucepan. Cook over medium heat, stirring constantly, until mixture boils. Pour over popcorn; toss well to coat. Bake, stirring frequently, for 30–40 minutes. Cool slightly in pan; remove to prepared serving plate. Store in airtight container for up to two weeks.

Candied Apples

1⅔ c cinnamon red hot candies
12 craft sticks

2 tbsp water
12 apples

Insert craft sticks into apples. Line a baking sheet with waxed paper. Pour candies and water in a heavy-bottomed saucepan over medium-high heat. Occasionally brushing down sides of pan with a heat-resistant pastry brush, heat candy to 300–310°, or until a small amount of syrup dropped into cold water forms hard, brittle threads. Remove from heat and let cool slightly. Dip apples into hot liquid and place on waxed paper to harden.

Chocolate Orange Truffles

¹/₄ c unsalted butter
3 tbsp heavy whipping cream
4 1-oz squares semisweet
   chocolate, chopped
2 tbsp orange juice

1 tsp orange peel, grated
4 1-oz squares semisweet
   chocolate, chopped
1 tbsp vegetable oil

In a medium saucepan, bring butter and cream to a boil over medium-high heat. Remove from heat. Add 4 squares chocolate, orange juice, and orange peel; stir until melted and smooth. Pour truffle mixture into a shallow bowl or a 9x5-inch loaf pan. Chill until firm, about 2 hours. Line 2 baking sheets with waxed paper. Shape chilled truffle mixture by rounded teaspoons into small balls. Place on prepared baking sheets. Chill until firm, about 30 minutes.

In top of a double boiler set over simmering (not boiling) water, heat remaining chocolate and oil, stirring until melted and smooth. Transfer chocolate mixture to a bowl. Cool completely. Drop truffles into melted chocolate mixture. Using 2 forks, lift out truffles, tapping gently on side of bowl to allow excess coating to drip back in bowl. Return truffles to baking sheets lined with waxed paper and chill until set.

Clothesline Candy

3 c sugar
½ c corn syrup
2 tbsp butter

1 c dates
1 c nuts
1 tsp vanilla extract

Mix first 3 ingredients and cook to medium-ball stage (244–248°). Remove from heat. Add dates and nuts. Boil 3 minutes. Remove from heat and let sit until almost cool. Add vanilla. Beat like fudge. Have dishtowel soaking in ice water. Pour candy onto wrung-out wet towel. Roll back and forth into roll. Roll up in towel. Tie each end with a string. Hang from clothesline to harden overnight. Take out of towel and slice.

Cracker Candy

½ lb butter
¾ c sugar
¼ of a 16-oz pkg saltine crackers

2 c semisweet chocolate chips
¾ c walnuts, chopped

Preheat oven to 425°. Melt butter in a saucepan over medium heat. Add sugar and stir occasionally until mixture comes to boil. Boil for 3 minutes and stir to keep from burning. Place crackers on a cookie sheet and drizzle with sugar mixture. Bake for 5 minutes or until edges begin to brown. Remove from oven and sprinkle chocolate chips on top, spreading them out as they melt. Sprinkle nuts on top and gently press into chocolate. Allow to cool and break into pieces. Refrigerate until ready to serve.

Chocolate Brittle Surprise

35 unsalted soda crackers
1 c butter
1 c brown sugar, packed

2 c semisweet chocolate
chips
1 c pecans, chopped
(optional)

Preheat oven to 350°. Cover cookie sheet with foil. Spray foil with cooking oil spray. Place crackers on foil in 5x7-inch rows. Microwave butter on high for 2 minutes. Add brown sugar and stir. Microwave on high for 2 more minutes, stirring every 30 seconds.

Pour over crackers. Bake 17–20 minutes (should bubble but not burn). Sprinkle chocolate chips over hot crackers. Spread after 2 minutes (chips have softened). Sprinkle nuts on top. Refrigerate 1 hour. Break into pieces. Can be frozen.

Peanut Butter Cups

2–3 lb melting chocolate
1 c graham cracker crumbs
(7½ whole crackers)

2 sticks butter, melted
¾ c peanut butter
1 lb box confectioners'
sugar

Coat small paper cup liners with melted chocolate to cup edge. Chill. Mix remaining ingredients; add mixture and cover with chocolate. Chill until firm.

Christmas Crunch

2 c sugar
⅔ c light corn syrup
½ c water
3 tbsp butter

1 tsp vanilla extract
½ tsp baking soda
2 c crispy rice cereal
1 c cashews

Grease one 10x15-inch baking pan. In a large saucepan over medium heat, combine sugar, corn syrup, and water; bring to a boil, stirring constantly until sugar is dissolved. Continue to cook, without stirring, until candy thermometer reads 300°. Remove from heat; stir in butter, vanilla, and baking soda. Add cereal and cashews; pour into prepared pan and allow to cool. Break into pieces and store in airtight container.

Basic Butter Cream Fondant

*The following fondant recipe is used as
the filling for chocolate-covered candy.*

2 sticks butter (room
temperature)

2 lb confectioners' sugar
7 oz marshmallow cream

Mix all ingredients together with your hands, kneading until smooth.
Makes about 2 1/2 pounds of fondant.

Coat candy molds with chocolate flavor of choice. Place small amount
of fondant on chilled chocolate. Coat with chocolate to seal, then chill.

Variations:
CHOCOLATE CREAM:

1/3 recipe Butter Cream
    Fondant

1/4 c cocoa

PEANUT BUTTER CREAM:

⅓ recipe Butter Cream Fondant

¼ c creamy peanut butter

PEPPERMINT:

⅓ recipe Butter Cream Fondant

Peppermint flavoring to taste

MAPLE-NUT CREAM:

⅓ recipe Butter Cream Fondant
Maple flavoring to taste

½ c walnuts or pecans, finely chopped

CHERRY-NUT CREAM:

⅓ recipe Butter Cream Fondant
¼ c maraschino cherry pieces

Cherry juice
¼ c walnuts, chopped

Mix cut-up pieces of maraschino cherries, cherry juice for flavoring, and cut-up walnuts. If recipe is too runny, add more confectioners' sugar.

Hard Rock Candy

3¾ c sugar
1½ c light corn syrup
1 c water

2 tsp cinnamon oil
1 tsp red food coloring
Confectioners' sugar

Roll edges of two 16-inch square pieces of heavy-duty aluminum foil. Sprinkle foil very generously with confectioners' sugar. In a large heavy saucepan combine sugar, corn syrup, and water. Heat over medium-high heat, stirring constantly until sugar dissolves. Stop stirring and heat until a candy thermometer reads 300–310°. Remove from heat and stir in cinnamon oil and food coloring. Pour over prepared foil; let cool and harden. Crack into pieces and store in an airtight container.

Melt-In-Your-Mouth Toffee

1 lb butter or margarine
1 c sugar
1 c brown sugar, packed

1 c walnuts, chopped
2 c semisweet chocolate
   chips

In a heavy saucepan, combine butter and sugars. Cook over medium heat, stirring constantly until mixture boils. Boil to brittle stage, 300°, without stirring. Remove from heat. Pour nuts and chocolate chips into a 9x13-inch dish. Pour hot mixture over nuts and chocolate. Let mixture cool and break into pieces before serving.

Microwave Peanut Brittle

1 c raw peanuts
1 c sugar
1/2 c light corn syrup
1/8 tsp salt

1 tsp butter
1 tsp vanilla extract
1/2 tsp baking soda

Mix peanuts, sugar, syrup, and salt in a 1 1/2-quart glass casserole dish. Microwave on high for 8 minutes, stirring after 4 minutes. Stir in butter and vanilla, then cook for 2 more minutes. Stir in baking soda. Pour onto a greased baking sheet. Using two forks, stretch until thin. Cool, then break into pieces.

Christmas Turtle Candies

4 oz pecan halves
24 caramels

1 c semisweet chocolate
   chips
1 tsp shortening

Preheat oven to 300°. Cover cookie sheet with aluminum foil, shiny side up. Lightly grease foil with vegetable oil spray. Place 3 pecan halves in a Y shape on foil. Place 1 caramel candy in center of each Y. Repeat. Bake just until caramel is melted, about 9–10 minutes. Heat shortening and chocolate chips over low heat just until chocolate is melted. Spread over candies and refrigerate for 30 minutes.

Christmas Lollipops

1 lb white chocolate, broken
   into small pieces
¼ c walnuts, finely chopped
1 tsp unsalted butter

36 candy stick molds
36 swizzle sticks (or
   candy sticks)

Combine chocolate and nuts in a stainless-steel bowl over a pan of simmering water. Stir mixture with a wooden spoon until chocolate melts and is creamy and smooth. Add butter and stir to melt. Spoon about 1 tablespoon of mixture into molds fitted with sticks. Smooth out top of each candy with a thin knife. Chill until candy sets, 2–3 hours. Remove candy from molds and store in layers of parchment or waxed paper in an airtight container. Will keep for up to 2 weeks.

Rocky Road Squares

3 lb milk chocolate
$\frac{1}{2}$ lb butter, softened

10 oz miniature marshmallows
3 lb peanuts

Melt chocolate; stir until smooth. Add butter and mix well (will be thick but warm). Set in cold place until it thickens around edges. Stir occasionally while cooling. Bring into warm room and stir 5–10 minutes until creamy and thinner. Add marshmallows and peanuts. Pour onto waxed paper-lined cookie sheet; press $\frac{3}{4}$ inch thick. Cool. Cut in squares at room temperature.

No-Fuss Caramel Corn

(for microwave)

3 qt popcorn, popped
1 c brown sugar, packed
$\frac{1}{2}$ c butter or margarine

$\frac{1}{4}$ c light corn syrup
$\frac{1}{4}$ tsp salt
$\frac{1}{2}$ tsp baking soda

Place popcorn in large brown paper bag; set aside. Combine sugar, butter, corn syrup, and salt in 2-quart glass bowl. Microwave on high 3–4 minutes, stirring after each minute. Microwave 2 more minutes. Stir in baking soda. Pour over popcorn in bag. Close bag and shake well. Microwave 1 minute and shake again. Microwave on high 1 minute more, shake well, and pour onto 2 cookie sheets. Cool and stir to separate popcorn.

White Chocolate-Covered Pretzels

6 1-oz squares white chocolate
1 15-oz pkg mini twist pretzels
¼ c red and green candy sprinkles

Melt white chocolate in top of a double boiler, stirring constantly. Dip pretzel halfway into white chocolate, completely covering half of the pretzel. Roll in sprinkles if desired, and lay on waxed paper. Continue process until all of the white chocolate is finished. Place in refrigerator for 15 minutes to harden. Store in airtight container.

Peanut Butter Fudge

2 c sugar
½ c milk
1½ c peanut butter
1 jar (7 oz) marshmallow cream

In a saucepan, bring sugar and milk to a boil. Boil for 3 minutes. Add peanut butter and marshmallow cream; mix well and fast. Quickly pour into a buttered pan. Size of pan is according to how thick you like your fudge. Chill until set. Cut into squares.

Peanut Patties

2 1/2 c sugar
1 c milk
2/3 c light corn syrup

Pinch of salt
4 c raw peanuts

Boil to soft-ball stage. Add:

4 tbsp butter
1/2 tsp vanilla extract

1 1/2 c confectioners' sugar
Red food coloring

Mix well. Drop by teaspoonfuls onto waxed paper.

Cookies

"Therefore I TELL YOU,

DO NOT WORRY ABOUT YOUR LIFE,

WHAT YOU WILL EAT OR DRINK;

OR ABOUT YOUR BODY,

WHAT YOU WILL WEAR.

IS NOT LIFE MORE IMPORTANT THAN FOOD,

AND THE BODY MORE

IMPORTANT THAN CLOTHES?"

MATTHEW 6:25

Snowflakes

1 c butter-flavored shortening
1 3-oz pkg cream cheese,
    softened
1 c sugar
1 egg yolk

1 tsp vanilla extract
1 tsp orange peel
2 ½ c flour
½ tsp salt
¼ tsp ground cinnamon

Preheat oven to 350°. In a medium bowl, cream together shortening, cream cheese, and sugar. Beat in egg yolk, vanilla, and orange peel. Continue creaming until light and fluffy. Gradually stir in flour, salt, and cinnamon. Fill cookie press and form cookies on ungreased cookie sheet. Bake in preheated oven for 10–12 minutes. Remove from cookie sheet and cool on wire racks.

Christmas Chinese Chews

¾ c flour, sifted
1 c nuts, chopped
1 tsp baking powder
2 eggs

1 c sugar
1 pinch salt
1 pkg dates, chopped
1 tsp vanilla extract

Mix ingredients and bake in a 9x13-inch ungreased pan at 375° for 20 minutes. While hot, cut into ½-inch strips, ½-inch wide, and roll in granulated sugar.

Christmas Stars

³/₄ c butter, softened
1 c sugar
2 eggs
1 tsp vanilla extract
2¹/₂ c flour

1 tsp baking powder
¹/₄ tsp salt
¹/₄ c green decorator sugar
    (optional)
6 tbsp strawberry jam

In a large bowl, cream butter and sugar until light and fluffy. Gradually add eggs and vanilla. Mix well. Sift together flour, baking powder, and salt. Stir flour mixture into butter mixture until well blended. Refrigerate dough for 3 hours. Preheat oven to 350°. Grease several cookie sheets.

On a floured surface, roll out ¹/₂ of the dough at a time to ¹/₈-inch thickness. Cut dough into star shapes using a 3- to 4-inch star cookie cutter. Using a 1- to 2-inch star cookie cutter, cut a star into the center of half of the big stars. If desired, sprinkle colored sugar on cookies with center cut out. Put onto prepared cookie sheets about 1 inch apart, and bake for 6–8 minutes. After cookies cool completely, spread 1 teaspoon of jam in center of each cookie that does not have a star cut out in the middle. Place a cookie with a cutout on top of the layer of jam. Pack cookies in a covered tin to preserve freshness.

Christmas Spice Cookies

³/₄ c sugar
²/₃ c butter or margarine, softened
¼ c orange juice
½ c dark corn syrup
½ c dark molasses
4½ c flour

³/₄ c whole wheat flour
2 tsp ground ginger
1 tsp baking soda
1 tsp salt
½ tsp ground cloves
½ tsp ground nutmeg
½ tsp ground allspice

In a mixing bowl, cream sugar and butter. Blend in orange juice, corn syrup, and molasses. In a separate bowl, combine flours, ginger, baking soda, salt, cloves, nutmeg, and allspice. Add to creamed mixture; mix well. Chill 3–4 hours or overnight. Roll a portion of dough on a lightly floured surface to ¼-inch thickness. Cut into desired shapes. Place 2 inches apart on greased baking sheets. Repeat with remaining dough. Bake at 350° for 12–14 minutes. Cookies will be soft and chewy if baked 12 minutes, crunchy if baked longer.

Mexican Chocolate Sticks

1 c butter, softened
1½ c confectioners' sugar
1 egg
1 tsp vanilla extract

1 tsp cinnamon
2 envelopes (1 oz each)
    premelted chocolate
2½ c flour

Mix butter and sugar. Add egg, vanilla, cinnamon, and chocolate. Blend in flour. With star plate in cookie press, form 4-inch fingers on an ungreased baking sheet. Bake at 375° for 5 minutes, or until set. Cool.

CHOCOLATE GLAZE:

1 c confectioners' sugar
1 envelope premelted chocolate

2 tbsp (or more) milk
Colored sprinkles

Blend first 3 ingredients; drizzle over cookies. Top with colored sprinkles.

Chocolate Snowballs

1¼ c butter
⅔ c sugar
1 tsp vanilla extract
2 c flour

⅛ tsp salt
½ c cocoa powder, unsweetened
2 c pecans, chopped
½ c confectioners' sugar

In a medium bowl, cream butter and sugar until light and fluffy. Stir in vanilla. Sift together flour, salt, and cocoa; stir into creamed mixture. Mix in pecans until well blended. Cover, and chill for at least 2 hours.

Preheat oven to 350°. Roll chilled dough into 1-inch balls. Place on ungreased cookie sheets about 2 inches apart. Bake for 20 minutes in preheated oven. Roll in confectioners' sugar when cooled.

Pecan Tassies

½ c butter
1 3-oz pkg cream cheese

1 c flour

Cream butter and cream cheese. Add flour; refrigerate 1 hour. Form into 24 small balls and press into small muffin tins.

FILLING:

¾ c brown sugar
1 egg, well beaten
1 tbsp butter, melted

1 tsp vanilla extract
Pinch of salt
¾ to 1 c pecans, chopped

Pour filling mixture into shells. Bake at 350° for 25 minutes.

Bon-Bon Christmas Cookies

4 oz cream cheese
½ c butter-flavored shortening
2 c flour, sifted

1½ c confectioners' sugar, sifted
2 10-oz jars maraschino cherries, drained

In a medium bowl, stir together cream cheese and shortening until well blended. Stir in flour, using your hands, if needed, to help it form a dough. If mixture seems too dry, add a couple of teaspoons of water. Cover and chill several hours or overnight.

Preheat oven to 375°. Lightly grease cookie sheets. Before rolling out dough, dust rolling surface heavily with confectioners' sugar. Roll dough out to ⅛-inch thickness. Cut into 1x4-inch strips. Place a cherry on end of each strip. Roll up each strip starting with the cherry. Place on prepared cookie sheets and dust with a little confectioners' sugar. Bake for 7–10 minutes in preheated oven. Cookies should brown slightly. Dust again with confectioners' sugar. Allow cookies to cool before serving, as cherries are very hot!

Christmas Logs

8 c flour
1 (^{1}/$_4$-oz) pkg active dry
    yeast
2 c butter or margarine
3 egg yolks
1 egg
2 c heavy whipping cream
1 tsp salt

1 tbsp vanilla extract
3 egg whites
4 c walnuts, ground
1^1/$_3$ c sugar
2 tbsp ground cinnamon
2 tbsp bread crumbs,
    dried
Sugar (for sprinkling)

Combine flour, yeast, and butter or margarine by hand until mixture is crumbly. Stir in egg yolks, egg, heavy cream, salt, and vanilla. Mix together and let stand in refrigerator for 8 hours or overnight.

Beat egg whites until stiff peaks are formed. In a separate bowl, mix walnuts, sugar, cinnamon, and bread crumbs. Stir in egg whites and let filling stand for 1 hour.

Divide dough into fourths. On a surface sprinkled with white sugar, roll ^{1}/$_4$ of dough out very thin (you should be almost able to see through the dough) into a rectangular or square shape. Spread ^{1}/$_4$ of the filling over rolled dough. Cut dough into 2^1/$_2$x2^1/$_2$-inch squares. Roll each square up like a jelly roll and place on a baking sheet. Repeat with remaining dough and filling. Keep dough you aren't working with in refrigerator. Bake at 350° for 20 minutes. Keep a close eye on these cookies as they tend to burn easily because of the sugar coating.

Holly Berry Cookies

2 c flour
1 c sugar
1 tsp ground cinnamon
³/₄ tsp baking powder
¹/₄ tsp salt
¹/₂ c butter, chilled
1 egg
¹/₄ c milk

²/₃ c seedless raspberry
    jam
2 c confectioners' sugar
2 tbsp milk
¹/₂ tsp vanilla extract
¹/₄ c cinnamon red
    hot candies
4 drops green food
    coloring

In a large bowl combine flour, sugar, ground cinnamon, baking powder, and salt. Cut in butter until mixture resembles coarse crumbs. In a small bowl, beat egg and ¹/₄ cup milk. Add to crumb mixture until dough is moistened. Cover and refrigerate for at least 1 hour.

Preheat oven to 375°. On a lightly floured surface, roll out dough to ¹/₈ inch thick. Cut with a 2-inch round cookie cutter. Place on ungreased baking sheets. Bake for 8–10 minutes or until edges are lightly browned. Cool on wire racks. Once cool, spread jam on half of the cookies, then top each with another cookie.

GLAZE:

Combine confectioners' sugar, 2 tablespoons milk, and vanilla until smooth. Spread glaze over cookie and decorate with red cinnamon candy before glaze is set. Let dry. Using a small, new paintbrush and green food coloring, paint holly leaves on cookies.

Fruit Foldovers

2 c flour
¼ c sugar
⅛ tsp salt
1 8-oz pkg cream cheese
1 c butter

1 c crushed pineapple
  pie filling
1 c confectioners' sugar
½ tsp rum-flavored extract
1½ tbsp water
2 tsp light corn syrup

In a large bowl, mix flour, sugar, and salt. Cut in cream cheese and butter until mixture resembles coarse crumbs. Work dough with hands until it holds together. Divide dough into four balls, wrap in waxed paper, and refrigerate for 2 hours or until dough is firm.

On a lightly floured surface, roll one of the dough balls into a 10-inch circle. Use a 3-inch cutter to cut dough into circles. Place ½ teaspoon of pie filling in center of each circle. Moisten edge of dough and fold over. Seal edge by pressing with the tines of a fork dipped in flour. Place on an ungreased baking sheet. Repeat with remaining dough. Bake at 350° for 20–25 minutes or until golden brown. Once cool, drizzle with glaze.

GLAZE:

Combine confectioners' sugar, rum flavoring, water, and corn syrup. Mix until smooth. Keep covered until ready to use.

Plum Jam Cookies

8 oz butter
1 c brown sugar, packed
1 egg
¼ c water

3 c flour
1 pinch salt
1 tsp baking powder
1 c plum (or any other
flavor) jam

In a large bowl, cream together butter and brown sugar. Beat in egg
and water. Sift together flour, salt, and baking powder; stir into butter mixture until well blended. On a lightly floured surface, roll out
dough to ¼-inch thickness. Cut with a 2-inch round cookie cutter.
Put half of the cookies onto a cookie sheet and spread ½ teaspoon of
plum jam in center of each one. With a thimble, or small cookie cutter, cut center out of remaining cookies. Place these on top of jam-
topped cookies to make sandwiches. Press together. Bake cookies at
375° for 10 minutes, then remove to a rack to cool.

Gingerbread People

4 c flour, sifted
1 tbsp ground cinnamon
2 tsp baking powder
1½ tsp ground ginger
1½ tsp ground cloves
1 tsp baking soda
1 tsp ground nutmeg

1 tsp salt
1 c unsalted butter (not margarine), room temperature
1 c sugar
2 large eggs, separated
1 c molasses
1 tbsp cold water

OPTIONAL DECORATIONS:

Currants for eyes
Strips of candied cherries for smiles

Red hot cinnamon candies for buttons

ICING:

2½ c confectioners' sugar, sifted
½ tsp vanilla extract

3–4 tbsp cold water
Assorted food colors

Onto a piece of waxed paper, sift 3¾ cups flour, cinnamon, baking powder, ginger, cloves, baking soda, nutmeg, and salt. In a large bowl, with an electric mixer on high, cream butter and sugar until light yellow and fluffy. Beat in egg yolks, one at a time, then molasses. Using a wooden spoon, stir in flour mixture. Cover and refrigerate dough for at least 1 hour or overnight.

Preheat oven to 350°. Butter three baking sheets. On a pastry cloth or board, sprinkle remaining ¼ cup flour and roll out half of the dough, ¼ inch thick. With cookie cutters, cut out gingerbread people. With a spatula, transfer them back to baking sheets. Decorate with currants, cherries, and cinnamon candies if you wish. In a cup, whisk egg whites with water. Bake cookies for 5 minutes, then brush lightly with egg white mixture. Bake 2–3 minutes more. Let cool on baking sheets for 2 minutes. (To make holes for hanging, pierce top of each cookie with a skewer as soon as it comes out of the oven.) With a spatula, transfer to racks to cool. Repeat with remaining dough and flour.

TO MAKE ICING:

In a small bowl, stir sugar with vanilla, then add enough water to make a stiff icing. Divide into small cups and color as you wish. When cookies are cold, pipe out designs, such as smiling faces, zigzags, bow ties, and aprons. If using different colors of icing, let one color dry before piping next. Store cookies in an airtight container for up to 2 weeks. Do not freeze, as icing could crack.

Orange Shortbread Fingers

³/₄ c flour
3 tbsp cornstarch
¹/₄ c plus 2 tbsp sugar

1 orange peel, grated
¹/₄ tsp salt
7 tbsp unsalted butter, chopped

Preheat oven to 300°. Grease an 8-inch square pan. Into a medium bowl, sift flour and cornstarch. Add ¹/₄ cup sugar, orange peel, and salt.

Using your fingertips, work butter into dry ingredients until mixture resembles fine crumbs. Knead mixture until it forms a dough, then press it into prepared pan. Score dough into 24 narrow rectangles and prick with the tines of a fork. Sprinkle with 2 tablespoons of sugar. Bake for 30 minutes or until a pale golden color. Remove from oven and leave shortbread to cool in pan until it holds its shape enough to turn out on a rack. When completely cooled, cut shortbread into fingers along the scored lines. The cookies can be stored in an airtight container for up to 1 week.

Surprise Packages

1 c butter
1 c sugar
½ c brown sugar
2 eggs
1 tsp vanilla extract

3 c flour
1 tsp baking soda
¼ tsp salt
48 thin-layered chocolate
    mint wafers

Cream butter and sugars until light and fluffy. Beat in eggs and vanilla. In a separate bowl, combine dry ingredients. Gradually add to creamed mixture. Mix well. Divide dough in half; wrap each in plastic wrap and refrigerate 1–2 hours. Preheat oven to 375°. Work with ½ the dough at a time. Using a scant tablespoon of dough, cover each mint, forming a rectangular-shaped cookie. Bake 10–12 minutes. Cool. Can be decorated with icing to look like a wrapped package.

No-Bake Sweets

"Who then is
THE FAITHFUL AND WISE SERVANT,

WHOM THE MASTER HAS PUT IN CHARGE OF

THE SERVANTS IN HIS HOUSEHOLD TO GIVE THEM

THEIR FOOD AT THE PROPER TIME?"

MATTHEW 24:45

Cherry Surprises

½ c butter, softened
1¾ c confectioners' sugar
1 tsp orange juice

1½ c coconut, shredded
1 10-oz jar maraschino cherries,
    drained

In a medium bowl, cream together butter, confectioners' sugar, and orange juice; mix in coconut. Wrap coconut mixture around each cherry to cover completely. Store in refrigerator in a tightly covered container until ready to serve.

Peanut Butter Balls

½ c peanut butter
½ c honey or corn syrup
¾ c nonfat dry milk

1 c crispy cereal flakes
Coconut or chopped nuts

Mix peanut butter and honey or corn syrup in a bowl. Stir in dry milk. Stir in cereal. Roll mixture into ¾-inch balls. Roll balls in coconut or nuts. Put into a container and store in refrigerator.

Swedish No-Bake Chocolate Balls

3 sticks margarine
2 c sugar
3 tbsp dark coffee (liquid)
3 tbsp cocoa

3 tsp vanilla extract
5 c quick oats
Coconut and colored sprinkles

Mix all ingredients in a bowl and form into ¾-inch balls. Dip in coconut and colored sprinkles. Refrigerate.

Christmas Orange Balls

4 c graham cracker crumbs
1 c confectioners' sugar
1 c pecans, chopped
¼ c light corn syrup

1 6-oz can frozen orange juice
    concentrate, thawed
¼ c butter, melted
⅓ c confectioners' sugar

In a medium bowl, stir together graham cracker crumbs, 1 cup confectioners' sugar, and pecans. Make a well in center and pour in corn syrup, orange juice concentrate, and melted butter. Mix well by hand until dough forms. Roll into 1-inch balls and roll balls in confectioners' sugar. Store at room temperature in an airtight container. Put a sheet of waxed paper between layers to prevent sticking.

Easy 5-in-1 No-Bake Cookies

BASE:

½ c peanut butter
½ c honey or corn syrup

¼ c orange juice
concentrate
1½ c nonfat dry milk

Mix thoroughly. Now choose one of the following 5 steps:

OATMEAL RAISIN:
2 c rolled oats   1½ c raisins

Mix into base. Shape into balls, then flatten.

CRISPY BALLS:
4 c crispy cereal

Mix into base. Shape into small balls.

RAISIN CLUSTERS:

¹/₄ c cocoa   4 c raisins

Mix into base. Form into small balls.

COCOA BALLS:

¹/₄ c cocoa   ¹/₄ c peanuts, chopped
2 c rolled oats   1 tsp vanilla extract

Mix into base. Shape into balls.

GRAHAMIES:

¹/₄ c raisins

Mix into base. Spread between graham crackers.

Peanut Butter Snacks

1 3-oz can Chinese noodles
1 c miniature marshmallows

1 6-oz pkg butterscotch chips
½ c peanut butter

Put noodles and marshmallows into large mixing bowl. Tear 2 large pieces of aluminum foil and lay on flat surface. Melt chips and peanut butter in double boiler over boiling water or in heavy pan. Stir until smooth. Pour mixture over Chinese noodles and marshmallows and mix (like popcorn balls). Spoon out by tablespoonfuls onto foil. Cool in refrigerator until hard.

No-Bake Peanut Butter Bars

2 c graham cracker crumbs
2 c peanut butter

1 lb confectioners' sugar
½ lb margarine or butter

Combine in mixing bowl and spread in ungreased 9x13-inch pan. Prepare frosting as follows.

FROSTING:

¼ c margarine

6 oz semisweet chocolate chips

Melt together. Spread over bars. Refrigerate; cut into squares.

Chocolate-Covered Orange Balls

1 lb confectioners' sugar
1 12-oz pkg vanilla
   wafers, crushed
1 c walnuts, chopped

¼ lb butter
1 6-oz can frozen orange
   juice concentrate, thawed
1½ lb milk chocolate, melted

In a large bowl, combine confectioners' sugar, vanilla wafers, walnuts, butter, and orange juice. Mix well and shape into 1-inch round balls; allow to dry for 1 hour. Place chocolate chips in top of double boiler. Stir frequently over medium heat until melted. Dip balls into melted chocolate and place in decorative paper cups.

No-Bake Peanut Oatmeal Drops

1 c sugar
¼ c butter
⅓ c evaporated milk
1 c peanut butter

½ tsp vanilla extract
1 c rolled oats
½ c peanuts

Bring sugar, butter, and milk to a rolling boil. Boil for 3 minutes, stirring frequently. Remove from heat and stir in peanut butter, vanilla, rolled oats, and peanuts. Drop by teaspoonfuls onto waxed paper. Let stand until set.

Chocolate Balls

1 c peanut butter
¾ c confectioners' sugar
1 c graham cracker crumbs
2 c semisweet chocolate chips
3 1-oz squares semisweet chocolate, chopped
1 tbsp shortening

In a medium bowl, mix together peanut butter and confectioners' sugar until smooth. Stir in graham cracker crumbs until well blended. Form dough into 1-inch balls by rolling in your hands, or by using a cookie scoop. Melt semisweet chocolate chips, semisweet chocolate squares, and shortening in top half of a double boiler. Use a fork to dip balls into melted chocolate, and place on waxed paper to cool until set.

No-Bake Chocolate Peanut Butter Oatmeal Cookies

2 tbsp butter
$\frac{1}{4}$ c cocoa
$\frac{1}{2}$ c sugar
$\frac{1}{4}$ c milk (condensed or whole milk)
Dash salt

1 tsp vanilla extract
1 heaping tbsp peanut butter (add more to taste and increase oatmeal)
$1\frac{1}{2}$ c uncooked oatmeal

Microwave butter in a microwave-safe bowl for 15–30 seconds, until butter is melted. Add cocoa and blend until cocoa is dissolved into butter. Add sugar, milk, and salt. Blend well. Microwave on high for 1 minute, 10 seconds to bring to a full boil. (Should you need to microwave batter some more, do so in 10-second increments. You want a full boil, but it will continue to cook after it's removed from microwave. Heating too long can cause mixture to scorch.) Add vanilla, peanut butter, and oatmeal. Stir well. Drop by tablespoonfuls onto waxed paper and allow to cool.

*Fun
Christmas Sweets
to Make
or Give Away*

Through Jesus,
THEREFORE, LET US CONTINUALLY OFFER TO

GOD A SACRIFICE OF PRAISE—

THE FRUIT OF LIPS THAT CONFESS HIS NAME.

AND DO NOT FORGET TO DO GOOD

AND TO SHARE WITH OTHERS,

FOR WITH SUCH SACRIFICES GOD IS PLEASED.

HEBREWS 13:15–16

Cookie Jar Sugar Cookies

4 c flour
1 tsp baking powder
$\frac{1}{2}$ tsp baking soda

$\frac{1}{2}$ tsp salt
$\frac{3}{4}$ tsp ground nutmeg
$1\frac{1}{2}$ c sugar

Combine flour with baking powder, baking soda, salt, and nutmeg. In a clean 1-liter glass jar with a wide mouth, layer sugar followed by flour mixture. Press firmly in place and seal. Attach a card with the following instructions:

SUGAR COOKIES

In a large bowl, beat 1 egg with 1 cup softened butter or margarine until light and fluffy. At low speed of an electric mixer, add $\frac{1}{2}$ cup sour cream, 1 teaspoon vanilla, and contents of jar. Mix until combined, using hands if necessary. Cover dough and refrigerate for several hours or overnight. Remove dough from refrigerator. Preheat oven to 375°. Roll chilled dough out on a lightly floured surface to $\frac{1}{8}$ inch thick. Cut dough into desired shapes. Place on an ungreased cookie sheet and bake for 10–12 minutes.

Chocolate Chip Cookie Mix in a Jar

1 tsp salt
1 tsp baking soda
2 c flour

1 c brown sugar, packed
$\frac{1}{2}$ c sugar
$1\frac{1}{2}$ c semisweet chocolate chips

Mix salt and baking soda with flour, then layer remaining ingredients into a 1-quart, wide-mouth jar. Use scissors to cut a 9-inch circle from calico. Place over lid, and secure with rubber band. Tie on a raffia or ribbon bow to cover rubber band. Enclose a card with the following mixing and baking directions:

CHOCOLATE CHIP COOKIES

Preheat oven to 375°. In a large bowl, cream 1 cup of unsalted butter or margarine until light and fluffy. Beat in 1 egg and 1 teaspoon of vanilla. Mix in cookie mix. Drop teaspoonfuls of dough, spaced well apart, onto a greased cookie sheet. Bake for 8–10 minutes in preheated oven, or until lightly browned. Cool on wire racks.

Oatmeal Raisin Spice Cookie Mix in a Jar

1 c flour
1 tsp ground cinnamon
$\frac{1}{2}$ tsp ground nutmeg
1 tsp baking soda
$\frac{1}{2}$ tsp salt

$\frac{3}{4}$ c raisins
2 c rolled oats
$\frac{3}{4}$ c brown sugar, packed
$\frac{1}{2}$ c sugar

Mix together flour, ground cinnamon, ground nutmeg, baking soda, and salt. Set aside. Layer ingredients in the following order into a 1-quart, wide-mouth jar: flour mixture, raisins, rolled oats, brown sugar, and sugar. Firmly pack down each layer before adding next layer. Attach a tag with the following instructions:

OATMEAL RAISIN SPICE COOKIES

Preheat oven to 350°. Line cookie sheets with parchment paper. Empty jar of cookie mix into large mixing bowl. Add $\frac{3}{4}$ cup butter or margarine, softened. Stir in 1 slightly beaten egg and 1 teaspoon of vanilla. Mix until combined, using hands if necessary. Shape into balls the size of walnuts. Place on lined cookie sheets 2 inches apart. Bake for 11–13 minutes in preheated oven, or until edges are lightly browned. Cool 5 minutes on cookie sheet. Transfer cookies to wire racks to finish cooling.

Chocolate Chip Walnut Cookie Mix in a Jar

1 c flour
½ tsp baking powder
½ tsp baking soda
1¼ c rolled oats
1 1½-oz bar milk chocolate

½ c sugar
½ c brown sugar, packed
½ c walnuts, chopped
½ c semisweet chocolate chips

Use a funnel that has a 2-inch opening to layer nicely in jar. With wire whisk, mix flour, baking powder, and baking soda. Pour into jar; pack down level with heavy object. Mix oatmeal in a blender. Grate chocolate bar and mix into oatmeal. Pack on top of flour in jar. Add white sugar and pack down. Add brown sugar and pack down. Layer chopped nuts on top of brown sugar. Finish layering jar with mini or regular chocolate chips until even with the top (no more than ½ cup). Enclose a card with the following mixing and baking directions:

CHOCOLATE CHIP WALNUT COOKIES

Preheat oven to 375°. Spoon chocolate chips and nuts into small bowl; set aside. Spoon sugars into mixing bowl; add ½ cup margarine or butter, cream well. Add 1 egg and ½ teaspoon vanilla; mix well. Pour oatmeal and flour mixture from jar into bowl and mix thoroughly. Stir in chocolate chips and nuts. Roll into walnut-sized balls; place on slightly greased cookie sheet 2 inches apart. Bake for 8–10 minutes.

Brownie Mix in a Jar

1¼ c flour
1 tsp baking powder
1 tsp salt

⅔ c cocoa powder, unsweetened
2¼ c sugar
½ c pecans, chopped

Mix together flour, baking powder, and salt in a quart jar. Layer remaining ingredients in the order listed. Press each layer firmly in place before adding next layer. Wipe out the inside of jar with a dry paper towel after adding cocoa powder, so other layers will show through the glass. Attach a tag with the following instructions:

BROWNIES

Preheat oven to 350°. Grease and flour a 9x13-inch baking pan. Empty jar of brownie mix into a large mixing bowl, and stir to blend. Mix in ¾ cup melted butter and 4 eggs. Mix thoroughly. Spread batter evenly into prepared baking pan. Bake for 25–30 minutes in preheated oven. Cool completely in pan before cutting into 2-inch squares.

Butterscotch Brownies

2 c flour
1½ tbsp baking powder
¼ tsp salt

½ c coconut, flaked
¾ c pecans, chopped
2 c brown sugar, packed

To a 1-liter jar, add flour, baking powder, and salt; stir together, and pack down. Then add and pack down remaining ingredients in this order: coconut, pecans, brown sugar. Attach a label with the following instructions:

BUTTERSCOTCH BROWNIES

Preheat oven to 375°. Grease a 9x13-inch baking pan. Empty jar of brownie mix into a large mixing bowl; stir to break up lumps. Add ¾ cup softened butter, 2 beaten eggs, and 2 teaspoons of vanilla extract; mix until well blended. Spread batter evenly in prepared pan. Bake for 25 minutes. Allow to cool in pan before cutting into squares.

Be joyful in hope,

PATIENT IN AFFLICTION,

FAITHFUL IN PRAYER.

SHARE WITH GOD'S PEOPLE

WHO ARE IN NEED.

PRACTICE HOSPITALITY.

ROMANS 12:12–13

Holiday
GIFT IDEAS

*L*ike the wise men, we give because the Lord first gave to us. The homemade touch puts an extraspecial quality on any gift. Going the homemade route can save money, and it doesn't have to take lots of time. The best gifts, though, aren't those with high price tags or those at the top of the popularity list. They are the ones that come from the heart.

There are no great things,
only small things
with great love.
Happy are those.

MOTHER TERESA

Simply
Special Gifts

"Freely you have received, freely give."

Matthew 10:8

Memory Books

These are perfect gifts for the hard-to-buy-for relative. Purchase a small blank journal or autograph book and write down some special, funny, and heartwarming memories about the person you will give it to. If time allows, pass the book around to other relatives and friends, and have them contribute a short note. Embellish pages with stickers, drawings, small photos, and the like. It is sure to be a gift that will be cherished for years to come.

Family History Book

Put your computer to work. Scan old family photos. Get as many pictures of grandparents and notable relatives as you can find—showing them young and old. Arrange the pictures on pages, starting with the oldest, and type an explanation of who the person was, when and where they lived, and any unique information you can provide about them. Use the photos and descriptions to trace family history and pass on important family notes about faith, traditions, and health. Print the pages on paper with some weight and durability. Use a three-hole punch and bind the pages in a small, ringed binder, or have a print shop bind your booklet. Make multiple copies so each individual in the family has one.

Family Cookbook

Organize your recipe box and create a special gift in the process. Take all those old handwritten recipe cards, newspaper clippings, and flagged cookbooks, and type the recipes into your computer. Be sure to include a note with each recipe that states who made it stand out and how it became a family favorite. If you have a handwritten recipe from a special relative who is now deceased, you may want to photocopy or scan it to preserve the handwriting as a piece of history. You can even divide your recipes according to the cooks and include their pictures. Place the pages on durable paper and bind them in a ringed binder that can be added to as more recipes become family treasures.

Personal Touch Calendar

Take a store-bought calendar and add family birthdays, anniversaries, and events for a new family member. Or, use your computer to create your own calendar. Insert family pictures on special dates.

Family Photos

It sounds too easy and even a bit egotistical, but distant (and not-so-distant) relatives and friends love to receive pictures of you and your growing family. You don't have to go to the expense of a professional portrait. A good snapshot with a pretty background will do fine. Buy an inexpensive frame for it. Or, collect several snapshots from special occasions throughout the year and put together a small photo album.

Growth Chart

A tape measure
2 dowel rods ¼" to ½" in diameter and 18" long
1½ yds of plain fabric
A piece of nursery fabric with patterns that can be cut out
Fusible webbing

Cut the fabric 18 inches wide and 1½ yards long. Make a deep hem in the top and bottom of the fabric, leaving an opening to slip the dowels through. Sew the tape measure onto the fabric starting with the "1" at the bottom of the fabric and going straight up. Cut shapes and patterns from the printed fabric and iron them onto the plain fabric with fusible webbing. You might use fabric paint to put the child's name across the top. Insert dowels. Tie a length of string snuggly onto the ends of the top dowel for a hanger. When hung, the bottom of the tape measure will need to be even with the floor.

Name Plaque

Try your hand at calligraphy (or use your computer's fancy fonts), and write the recipient's name on special paper. (Find some with weight that's light in color—perhaps with pressed flowers in the grain or another subtle design.) Add the meaning of the name or a thoughtful poem. You could use your child's name and add his or her handprints as a great gift for grandparents.

The Personalized Touch

With a little fabric paint and/or stitching, the following items could be personalized with the recipient's name or a unique design. Add embellishments like sequins and buttons for an extraspecial touch.

Aprons	Place mats
Doormat	Pot holders
Gloves	T-shirts and sweatshirts
Napkins	Tennis shoes
Pillowcases	Towels

Personalized Pillowcase

Use muslin to make a simple case, or buy an inexpensive case. Place a sturdy piece of cardboard inside the case and use a pencil to lightly mark your design. Use fabric paint pens or permanent markers to create a colorful, personalized design. Write the recipient's name, a Bible verse, or blessing on the pillowcase and create simple flowers, vines, or shapes for decoration.

Personalized Scripture Cards

From Lena Nelson Dooley of Hurst, TX

"For I know the plans I have for you, Rebecca,"
declares the LORD,
"plans to prosper you and not to harm you,
plans to give you hope and a future."

JEREMIAH 29:11

Choose several Scriptures in which a name can be appropriately added. Write them on cards, or set them up with a computer and printer. Use small, uniform-sized cards that can be bundled with ribbon. For computer printing, try a sheet of business cards that are perforated for easy separation.

Fabric Button Earrings

From a fabric store, buy a kit for fabric-covered buttons. From a craft store, buy earring backs. Use scraps of pretty calico or a fancy but sturdy (though not thick) fabric. Follow the kit's instructions for making the button cover. Twist off the button loop with pliers. Glue the earring back to the center of the button's back with a heavy craft glue.

Simple Homemade Soap

A mold (specially bought plastic soap mold, cookie cutters, or even an ice cube tray)
Bar soap remains (mild soap like Ivory works well)
Grater
Water
Food coloring
Perfume or potpourri oil

Grate soap pieces into a powdery texture. Mix with just enough water to create a thick paste. Add a drop or two of food coloring and fragrance. Knead the mixture until it is thick like dough; press the mixture into a mold, or roll the soap into balls. Let it dry for at least 24 hours. For a simple gift, tie a ribbon around the homemade bars of soap or fill a small gift basket with little soap shapes.

Bath Bombs

In a glass bowl, mix 1 part citric acid (you can get this at a pharmacy) with 2 1/4 parts baking soda. Add several drops of essential oil and a few drops of food coloring. Moisten by spraying with water or witch hazel (witch hazel works better because it evaporates more quickly) until mixture just begins to stick together. Shape truffle-sized balls (1-inch diameter) of the mixture. Let the bombs dry and harden for 24–48 hours. Pack each bomb into its own paper candy cup. Store bombs in a closed container. To use, drop 1–3 into warm bath water.

Scented Bath Salts

2 c Epsom salts
1 c sea salt, rock salt, or coarse salt
Food coloring

1/4 tsp glycerin
4 or 5 drops essential oil for fragrance (vanilla, citrus, or peppermint)
(green or blue, optional)

Combine salts in a large glass or metal mixing bowl and mix well. Add food coloring, a few drops at a time, until desired color is achieved. For white salts, simply skip the coloring. Add glycerin and essential oil and mix well. Spoon salts into clean, dry jars with cork stoppers or metal screw-on lids and seal. Makes 3 cups of bath salts. When giving as a gift, attach a label identifying the scent and recommend using 1/3 to 1/2 cup in the bath.

Milk Bath Powder

1 c dry milk
5–8 drops scented oil (perfume oil or essential oil)

Combine dry milk with oil and mix well. The more oil used, the stronger the scent. Place in a pretty jar. Attach a card with directions: To use, add to running bath water. You'll come out soft and smelling good!

Rose Water

3 c rose petals, picked just after the morning
  dew has dried
3 c purified water

Place petals in a glass container and pour boiling water over the petals. Allow to steep for 2 days, stirring frequently. Strain. Pour into pretty bottles; seal, and give with a pretty identification card and ribbon attached.

Peppermint Skin Toner

1 pt vinegar   1 c mint leaves
1 pt purified water

Place all ingredients in a glass saucepan and bring to a boil. Remove from heat. Pour into a glass jar and allow to steep for 4 days. Strain and bottle in decorative containers. Label each container with a pretty identification card and ribbon.

Sinus Headache Pillows

Flax seeds   Eucalyptus leaves
Crushed spearmint leaves   Rosemary leaves
Crushed peppermint leaves $1/8$ yd cotton fabric
Whole lavender buds

Blend the herbs. Cut two pieces of fabric 4x10 inches and sew right sides together with a $1/4$-inch seam. Leave a 2-inch opening. Turn it right side out and stuff with the herb mixture. Sew opening closed. Tie a ribbon around the middle with a tag including directions to use as a reliever of headaches.

Herb Sachets

Cotton fabric cut into 4"x4" squares
1 handful each of dried lavender flowers and
    rosemary
1 tbsp of crushed cloves
Small pieces of dried lemon peel

Blend the herbs in a bowl. Place right sides of two fabric squares together and sew a $1/4$-inch seam, leaving a 1-inch opening. Turn the right sides out and stuff the square pouch with the herb mixture. Sew the opening closed. (Sew a loop of ribbon onto a few sachets so they can be hung over a clothes hanger.) Wrap several sachets together in tissue paper tied with raffia. Attach a note explaining that these should be placed in drawers, closets, and boxes to protect clothing from insects and to add freshness.

Pinecone Fire Starters

Several dry pinecones
Paraffin or old candle stubs
Candlewick
Scented oil (cinnamon, bayberry,
    or citrus spice)

Melt the wax in a coffee can placed in a pan of water. Add a few drops of oil to melted wax. Wrap or tie a length of wick around the top of each pinecone. Dip pinecones into melted wax several times, allowing wax to harden between dips. For gift-giving: Present them in a small basket with a note of instruction to add 2–3 pinecones to fire kindling and light the wicks.

Fragrant Draft Dodger

Buy ⅓ yard of 45-inch decorative calico. Trim it down to 38 inches long. Trim the short ends with pinking shears. On the long side, fold the right sides together and sew a ½-inch seam. Turn right side out. Gather the fabric at one end. About 3 inches in, secure with a rubber band, then fill the tube with dry potpourri. Stop about 3 inches from the end. Gather the fabric and secure with a rubber band. Tie raffia, jute, or ribbon over the rubber bands, and you're done. Place at the bottom of drafty doors.

Scented Notepaper

Plan at least one month ahead for this homemade gift. Buy fine-textured rice or petal paper. Fill a pretty gift box ¾ full of paper. Between every 3–4 sheets of paper, sprinkle a handful of flowers (freesia, lavender, orange blossom, or rose) or scented herbs. Cover the box and let it sit for 4 weeks. Remove the flowers and tie a satin ribbon around the stack of paper.

Mosaic Coaster

4" clay saucer
Small pieces of broken
   stained glass or colored tile
Heavy craft glue

1 thin sheet of cork
Acrylic paint
Tile grout

Paint the saucer—except for the bottom of the inside where the glass will be glued on. Allow paint to dry completely. Arrange pieces of glass on the bottom inside of the saucer, covering the entire area. When you have a pattern set, start gluing one piece at a time. Just a dab of glue will do. As the glue sets for about 30 minutes, prepare your grout. Spread the grout over all the glass and gently press it into the spaces between each piece. Let it set about 10 minutes; use a damp sponge to wipe extra grout from the surface of the glass and along the painted sides of the saucer. Allow the grout to dry overnight. The last step is to glue on a circle of cork that is just a bit smaller than the bottom of the saucer. As a finishing touch, you can apply a grout sealer to protect the white grout from stain.

Scented Coasters (and Trivets)

Prequilted material
Thread

Granulated potpourri
    from a paper sachet

Cut two 3–4-inch circles or squares from the prequilted material. Pin them together with right sides facing. Stitch them together, leaving a hole large enough to place potpourri. Turn stitched pieces right side out and press with a warm iron. Fill with potpourri. (You may want to make larger ones as trivets.) When you place a hot container or cup of tea on the coaster or trivet, the heat will activate the aroma.

Lighted Potpourri Jar

1 qt canning jar
1 string of 18–25 white
    Christmas lights

Potpourri
4"–6" lace or crocheted
    doily

Place the end of the light string that does not have the plug in the bottom of the jar. Add a handful of potpourri. Start winding the light string into the jar, stopping occasionally to add more potpourri. When the jar is full, let the cord with plug hang out and cover the top with the doily. Secure the doily in place by tying raffia or ribbon around the edge. When you plug this in, the low heat generated from the lights will warm the potpourri and fill the room with fragrance.

Jar Lamp

1 qt canning jar with lid
and ring
1 small hurricane lamp
shade with a base the
same diameter as the
jar's mouth
1 wick (the length of
the jar)

1 ceramic lamp oil
adapter available
from craft stores
with candle-making
supplies
Clear lamp oil
Large pieces of
potpourri

First, poke a hole in the center of the jar lid and set the adapter over the hole. Thread the wick through both holes. Fill a clean, dry jar with large pieces of potpourri (like dry orange slices, cinnamon sticks, pinecones, and whole cloves). Cover the contents completely with lamp oil. Set the lid on the jar, carefully pushing the wick down into the oil and potpourri. Tighten the ring down on the lid and set the hurricane shade in place.

Shaded Lamp

Buy an inexpensive lamp with a plain white shade. Use acrylic paints to stencil a design onto the shade. Or sponge-paint the shade, using 3 blending colors.

Umbrella Holder

Gather 3 three-pound coffee cans. Clean them and cut out the bottoms. Set the cans on top of each other and glue or solder the edges together. Measure the perimeter of a can and the height of the stack; then cut fabric for covering the cans completely. You can stitch cloth shapes onto the fabric for design. Use thick glue to attach the fabric to the cans.

Coffee Can Canisters

Collect 1- and 2-pound sizes of coffee cans with lids. Spray, brush-paint, or sponge-paint with enamel. Allow the paint to dry completely. Add decals, ribbon edges, and other designs that fit snug and flat against the can. Paint the words "flour," "sugar," and "salt" on the cans, if desired. Add several coats of clear spray coating so the canisters can be wiped clean.

Cheese Board

Buy a very smooth, nice piece of maple wood, 1-inch thick and 8–10 inches wide. Cut it into a square and sand the rough edges. Seal with varathane or other sealant. Give with a cheese knife or slicer.

Decorative Curtain

Any teen will enjoy this fun gift.

1 yardstick
1 big bag of neon-colored
    drinking straws

1 bag of colorful beads
1 skein of yarn

Take a yardstick (often given away by lumber companies) and drill a hole at every inch marker. Drill against a piece of scrap lumber to keep the yardstick from cracking. Paint the yardstick, then cut the yarn in 5–6-foot lengths, and tie one end of each length through a hole in the yardstick. Cut the straws in thirds (about 2 inches per section) and thread them onto the yarn. Add a bead (or even a fake flower) every so often. When you reach the bottom of the yarn, secure a large bead for weight. When done, the curtain should fit across the average doorway.

Exercise Mat

2 terry-cloth beach towels (approximately 28"x49")
A sheet of thick foam from a fabric or upholstery store
    cut 2" smaller than the size of one towel
2 elastic strips 30" long and 2" wide

Pin the towels together and stitch a $\frac{1}{4}$-inch seam, leaving an opening of at least 6 inches. Trim the corners and turn right sides out. Insert the foam. Hand-stitch the opening closed. For each piece of elastic, sew the ends together to make a circle. Use these elastic circles to slip over the mat when it is rolled.

Sweet Treats

Fill a canning jar with colorful candies. Tie a ribbon and tag around the neck of the jar, and you have an instant gift. Add a note tag that says "You are a real sweetie" or "I appreciate your sweet friendship." A jar could also be filled with small cookie cutters. Attach your favorite sugar cookie recipe.

Heating Bag

This little bag is very nice for soothing
little aches and pains or warming cold feet.

$1/2$ yd of flannel (cotton)
    fabric
18" of 1"-wide cotton webbing,
    cut into 2 equal pieces

4 c uncooked rice
1 tbsp whole cloves

Cut the flannel into a 14x18-inch rectangle. Fold, right sides facing, to 7x18 inches. Mark each short end at the fold with a straight pin; unfold. For handles: Pin one end of webbing 1 inch from the fold; pin remaining end $1^3/_4$ inches from the cut edge. Repeat for opposite handle on other short end. Fold fabric in half, right sides facing with handles sandwiched inside. Pin the edges allowing a $3/_4$-inch seam, and sew the bag together, leaving a 3-inch opening along the long side. Clip the corners and turn the bag right side out. Fill with rice and cloves, then hand-sew the opening closed. To use as a heating pad, microwave for 1–2 minutes on high. Remove from microwave, using the handles.

A Living Gift

Give a gift of a homegrown houseplant (or herbs you've cultivated from seeds). Take clippings from a hearty plant like an ivy, philodendron, or spider plant. Start them in a tin, a clay pot, a coffee mug, an old boot, a lined basket, or any unique pot. Keep soil moist until rooted. Attach plant care instructions with a ribbon.

Blossoming Bucket

Buy some spring bulbs for daffodils, tulips, or hyacinths, and put them in the coldest corner of your refrigerator for 2–4 weeks. Fill over half a bucket or large vase with gravel, pebbles, or marbles. Nestle the bulbs among the top pebbles, points facing upward. Add water just to the top of the pebbles. In a few weeks there will be blossoms for all to enjoy. Give the bucket away at any stage of the bulbs' growth.

Give Old Things New Life

- Old windows become mirrors. Just replace the glass panes with some mirrors cut to size by a glass shop.

- Torn or stained quilts can be remade into stuffed toys, small pillows, framed artwork, etc.

- Remove crystal drops from a broken or incomplete chandelier and use as tree ornaments.

- Put old doorknobs or drawer pulls in a line on a stained and varnished or painted board for a unique pegboard on which to hang coats or other items.

- Put a simple wooden top and base on a thick old porch or stair spindle and create a stand for a plant or lamp.

- Melt old candle stubs. Fill an old teacup or seashell with wax and wick.

- Any kind of container that has lost its lid—cookie jar, teapot, candy dish, etc.—can become a unique flowerpot.

- Old house shutters attached together with hinges can have new life. Use tall ones for a room divider and short ones for a fireplace screen.

Incredible Clay

¼ c household glue   Dab of acrylic paint
⅓ c cornstarch   (optional)

Make clay by mixing glue with cornstarch. Add a drop of paint if you want to color your clay. Stir together until flaky, then knead with hands until it turns to a smooth clay consistency. (Store clay in an airtight bag until ready to use.) Roll out clay with a rolling pin until it is ⅛-inch thick. Cut out shapes with cookie cutters, if desired, then let dry overnight. While clay is still damp, you can mold the shape and glue it against a picture frame or decorative can. You can also let the rolled-out clay dry out overnight and cut out shapes with scissors. Decorate with acrylic paints or permanent markers either while damp or when dry. It is incredibly versatile clay.

Kid's Dress-Up Chest

Buy a large, plastic storage box with lid. Paint the sides with fabric or acrylic paints. Use the child's name in your design. Then go to yard sales and thrift shops, collecting several pieces of unique clothing—like a wedding dress and veil, prom dresses, ballerina's tutu, uniforms, costumes, and the like. Also look for extravagant hats, shoes, purses, and jewelry. Fill the storage box, and give the gift of hours of imaginative fun.

*It is good to be children sometimes,
and never better than at Christmas,
when its mighty Founder was a child Himself.*

CHARLES DICKENS, *A Christmas Carol*

Kid-Involved Gifts

*"If you, then, though you are evil,
know how to give good gifts to your children,
how much more will your Father in heaven
give good gifts to those who ask him!"*

MATTHEW 7:11

A Special Bookmark

This one's sure to please Grandma and Grandpa! Gather old and new pictures of your family and trim them to fit on a piece of heavy paper that is approximately 2x7 inches. Arrange them on the front and back and secure in place with glue. You can add the date, a Scripture, or sentiment, etc. Have the bookmark laminated, or cover it with clear contact paper.

Photo Puzzle Cards

Get a large print made of a favorite family photo. Mount the photo to green or red poster board with spray adhesive or a light, even coating of glue. When dry, write a greeting on the back side. Help the child use scissors to cut the photo into 8–12 pieces. Place in an envelope and mail. (You may want to place the puzzle in a small plastic bag before placing it in the envelope.)

Puzzle Picture Frame

Pick up an old jigsaw puzzle or two from a garage sale (the more colorful the pieces the better). Fashion a square, triangle, or hexagon out of craft sticks by gluing them together. Then glue the jigsaw pieces on the sticks. Make a wide frame with enough space in the middle to attach a picture to the back. Cut out lightweight cardboard in the same size and shape as the stick frame, and glue it behind the picture. Attach string or ribbon to hang this ornament on your tree or attach a magnet for refrigerator displays. (Hot glue makes the project quick but requires supervision when children are involved.)

Silhouette Picture

Gather a flashlight, a large piece of heavy white paper, and a pen, pencil, or marker. Tape the paper to the wall. Have your child stand or sit sideways beside the paper. Darken the room and shine the flashlight on the child so the profile is shadowed on the paper. Trace the shadow; then cut out the profile and mount it on a contrasting piece of paper. This is striking with the profile cut out of black paper and mounted on white paper or vice versa.

Plaster Handprint

In a large disposable container, mix together 1 cup of water and $2\frac{1}{4}$ cups of plaster of paris until it is thick but pourable. Pour into an aluminum pie plate. When the plaster is firm enough to hold a shape, have the child press his or her hand into it and carefully lift up. Allow the child to press some marbles, seashells, or other small embellishments into the plaster, but leave the handprint untouched. Let the mold dry completely overnight. Record the date and the child's name on back.

Personalized T-Shirt

This needs adult supervision. Gather crayon shavings and bits, and place them in an emptied and cleaned soup can. (You will need a different can for each color used.) Place the can over a pan of boiling water until crayon is melted. Work quickly to paint pictures and words on a plain cotton T-shirt, apron, or glove (with cardboard protection underneath or between fabric layers). For permanent color, cover the design with a scrap of fabric or old towel and press with a hot iron.

No Skidding Socks

Buy a quality pair of thick socks. Trace the foot of the person you will give the socks to (or use the foot of someone of similar size) onto cardboard. Put the cardboard foot shape into the sock, then use fabric paint to decorate the bottom of the sock. When the paint is completely dry, put the sock in the dryer for 10–15 minutes in order to set the paint.

Scented Sachet

Cut a circle of lightweight fabric 8–10 inches in diameter. In the center, pile either rose petals; cotton balls with vanilla oil; cinnamon bark with orange peels and cloves; lemon thyme and lemon verbena leaves; or lavender flowers. Draw up the edge and tie with ribbon.

Fragrant Soap Balls

Ivory Snow Flakes   Perfume or scented oil
Food coloring

Use water to moisten the soap flakes to a consistency likened to very stiff dough. Divide the mixture into several bowls. Add a different perfume and food coloring to each bowl for variety. Have children shape large spoonfuls of the soap into balls. Place the balls on trays (labeled with their molder's name!) to harden for several days. Have each child wrap his or her soap balls in colored cellophane paper and tie the package with a pretty ribbon.

Quilted Pillows

For a good way to get children to learn simple sewing skills try this: Gather fabric scraps (preferably cotton) and cut 9 squares, approximately 4x4 inches. Help your child sew the pieces together by hand to form one 12x12-inch square (for younger children you might want to use only 4 squares that are 6x6 inches so there is less sewing to do). For the backside you can do another set of 9 squares, or you can choose one piece of fabric that measures 12x12 inches. Place both 12-inch square pieces with right sides facing and sew around the edges, leaving a small section open to flip it right side out. Fill with polyester stuffing and sew up the opening.

Decorative Light Switch Cover

Gather 9 Popsicle sticks (the amount used can vary with size of light cover), craft glue, a sheet of craft foam, and foam craft shapes. Use the existing light cover to cut the foam sheet to fit the switch area. Mark the center opening with a pen and use a utility knife to cut an opening in the center of the foam. Place one stick against the switch and mark where to cut the opening. An adult should help with the sharp scissors or a utility knife to cut the stick. Glue the sticks onto the foam, straight and touching. The sticks should hang over the edges of the foam just a bit to cover it. Decorate the switch cover with paint and foam shapes. When the switch cover is completely dry, use double-sided tape to attach it to the existing switch plate cover.

Pet Rock Paperweight

Glue two well-shaped rocks together to make the head and body of a duck, ladybug, or other creature. Add features with markers, bits of felt or fabric, pipe cleaners, wiggly eyes, and so on.

Glass Aquarium

Glass container
Glass fish with floats
Shells, stones, or marbles

Artificial greenery
Sand or decorative
  gravel

Select a fish bowl, a regular bowl, or a decorative bottle or jar for your aquarium. If you choose a glass container with a lid, it will require less cleaning and the water will not evaporate as quickly. Start with some sand or gravel on the bottom and anchor your greenery into it. Add some seashells or glass marbles for interest. Slowly pour water into the aquarium (you can color the water with food coloring), then add the floating glass fish.

CD Coaster

4–6 CDs (plain gold or
  silver CDs look best)

White cotton lace
Glue

Hold a CD in one hand and spread some glue along the outside edge. Take one end of the lace (don't cut it yet) and lay it along the glued edge, pleating it as you go. When you've gone all around, cut the lace to meet the starting end. The coaster is done and will hold heat well.

Pretzel Wreath

Use small pretzels (those that are almost heart shaped). Arrange one layer of them in a circle like a wreath, then glue a second layer on top of the first, joining the pretzels together over the middle of a pretzel on the first layer. Weave ribbon between the holes if you like. Hang with a ribbon.

Scoop of Hugs and Kisses

Laundry soap scoop
Hugs and Kisses candy

Clear or colored plastic
wrap
Ribbon

Fill the scoop with candy. Cut a large piece of plastic wrap and place the scoop in the middle. Draw the plastic wrap tightly around the scoop and gather it around the handle. Tie a ribbon around the handle to hold the wrap in place. Add a note that says, "Hugs and Kisses from me to you."

Snow Globe

Clean a glass jar that has a lid. (Small jam or peanut butter jars work well, but avoid the ones with the "fresh test button" on the lid.) Fill the jar with water, screw on the lid, and turn it upside down for awhile to see if the seal will hold water. Paint the outside of the lid with a coat or two of acrylic paint. Arrange a grouping of clean plastic (or otherwise waterproof) items on the inside of the lid. Glue them in place with a water-resistant glue. When the glue has dried, fill the jar with water and add approximately a teaspoon of gold or silver glitter. Put a tiny ribbon of glue around the inside edge of the lid and immediately screw the lid tightly onto the jar.

Glove Puppets

Buy inexpensive ladies' knit gloves. For each glove, gather five 1-inch pompoms and ten 5-millimeter wiggle eyes. You'll also need thick craft glue and 5 tongue depressors. Each pompom will be a head. First glue the eyes in place. A tiny pompom or sequin can be added for a nose. Ears made of felt can be glued to the back. Be creative with embellishments. Before putting the head onto the end of the glove finger, insert a tongue depressor inside the finger and allow the glue to set before removing the stick.

Spoon Puppets

Gather wooden spoons and embellishments like 7-millimeter wiggle eyes, foam shapes, fabric and ribbon remnants, paint, and markers, including hot or craft glue. Start by painting your spoon. The back of the spoon will be the face area. You may want flesh color above where the spoon narrows to the handle and a bright color along the handle. Set eyes in place with glue. Use a sharp permanent marker to add a smile. Cut small circles out of foam for cheeks, nose, and ears. Glue in place. Tie ribbon to the "neck." Use thin strips of fabric or ribbon for "hair." Be creative.

To make a snowman: Paint your spoon all white. Set eyes in place. Use a long teardrop-shaped orange foam piece for nose and small circles of foam in red or pink for cheeks. Paint a 2-inch straw hat black and add a holiday ribbon to the neck for a scarf.

Turtle Trinket Box

2 clay saucers, 4" in diameter   Small foam ball
4 clay pots 1½" tall   2 wiggle eyes

Paint the saucers and pots with acrylic paint (green is great for this project). You can add a shell design to one saucer that will be used on the top side of the turtle's shell. Paint some toes on the clay pots on the outside edges with the opening facing down. Paint the foam ball, adding face detail as you like. Allow the paint to dry. Use heavy craft glue to attach the foam ball to the saucer that will be the top, facedown. Place the bottom saucer facedown on your table, then glue the bottom of the pots to the bottom of the saucer. When dry, place the rims of the saucers together. The top lifts off when you are ready to place trinkets inside.

"Most Special" Gift Box

Paint or cover the outside of a shoebox with paper and decorate. Keep the lid separate and removable. Secure a small mirror onto the bottom of the inside of the box. Make a card that reads something like "The person pictured here is one of the most special gifts in my life." Glue it on the inside of the box top.

Decoupaged Bottles

Colorful tissue paper
White glue
Paintbrush

Clean, clear glass or
plastic bottles, jars,
vases, or bowls

Make sure whatever you are decoupaging is clean, dry, and dust-free. Rip or cut tissue paper into different shapes. Water down the glue just a bit. Brush glue on small areas of object you are decoupaging. Place colored tissue in desired pattern. Paint a little more glue on top of tissue. Let dry. It's best to work on a protected surface. Place gifts like a candle, bath salts, or homemade potpourri inside the finished bottles.

Homemade Decorations to Share

*"We will share with you
whatever good things
the* LORD *gives us."*

NUMBERS 10:32

Fabric Garland

Scraps of cotton Christmas fabric and even some plain colors and muslin

Twine, jute, or heavy string

Cut a length of twine at least 6 feet long. Tie a loop in one end. Cut fabric in strips measuring 1x6 inches. Tie the fabric onto the twine—knot in the middle and equal amount of fabric on both sides. Alternate fabrics as you go. Keep the pieces close together for a full effect to your garland.

You'll want at least 24 feet for an average 6-foot tree. You can also drape this garland across your curtain rods or around your banister.

Candy Train Engine

A great ornament or place favor.

Glue a roll of ring-shaped candy to the wide side of a package of gum. Glue 4 round peppermint candies to the bottom against the gum pack for wheels. Make a loop of narrow ribbon and glue the ends to the top of one end of the candy roll. Glue a caramel on top of the ribbon ends for an engineer's cab. To the other end of the candy roll, glue a chocolate kiss for a smokestack and another kiss on the same end of the package of gum for a plow front.

Rag Tree

A straight twig 8–14" long and as thick as a kinder-
gartner's pencil
A base out of a branch 1½" tall and 2" in diameter
⅛ yd of cotton fabric in Christmas color
24–36 tiny pinecones no more than a ¼" tall

Whittle the smallest end of the twig to a point. Match a drill bit to the
other end of the twig and drill a hole in the base piece at least 1 inch
deep. Glue the twig into the hole. Cut strips of fabric with pinking
shears, ¾-inch wide by 6 inches long. Tie the first strip just below the
pointed tip of the twig. Add strips, keeping them close and altering the
direction the ends hang. When the twig is full, use the pinking shears
to trim the ends of the fabric to vary the lengths—longest at bottom to
shortest at top. Glue a small pinecone to the end of each fabric strip.

Scented Tree Ornaments

1 c applesauce	2 tbsp nutmeg	2 tbsp ground
¾ c cinnamon	2 tbsp ginger	cloves

Mix all ingredients together. Roll onto waxed paper to ⅛-inch thickness. Cut out with cookie cutters. Poke holes for hangers with a drinking straw. Put on a wire rack and allow to dry for 3 days, turning daily.
Use fabric paints, sequins, and other embellishments to dress them up.
Makes approximately 1 dozen ornaments.

Candy-Coated Ornaments

Buy several small foam balls. Spread a coating of glue over the ball and glue on your favorite candy. Red cinnamon candies, crushed peppermint sticks, round peppermints glued on their narrow sides, gumdrops, M&Ms, or any other fun candy will work (best to use just one variety of candy per ball). Use a long straight pin to secure a loop of ribbon to the top for a hanger.

Cookie Cutter Photo Ornaments

Trim a favorite photo to fit inside a cookie-cutter shape. Glue the edges of the picture to the inside of the cutter. You can add ribbon, lace, glitter, and paint to the cutter as desired. Remember to label the picture with name and date. Hang on the tree. Make a collection of these ornaments to show the growth of a child or changes in the family's appearance over the years. (A great gift for Grandma!)

Sparkling Ornaments

Trace cookie-cutter shapes onto plain paper. Place waxed paper over the design and outline it with glue. Coat the surface of the shape with glue and fill it with glitter (the ultrafine variety works best). Let dry for several days. Cut out the shape and repeat glue and glitter on the reverse side. When completely dry, make a hole in the top and create a hanger with thread or thin ribbon.

Fabric-Fused Wooden Ornaments

From a craft store, buy simple wooden shapes cut from $\frac{1}{8}$-inch plywood (stars, trees, bells, etc.). Sand the rough edges and wipe them clean. Lay an old towel or sheet over your ironing board. Spread a large piece of holiday fabric (cotton) out on the ironing board facedown. Place a matching-sized sheet of fusible web on it with paper side up. Cover with a thin towel and use a hot iron to press the webbing on according to the directions. When cool, peel the paper away. Set your wooden shapes on the covered ironing board. Keep them close together (about $\frac{1}{2}$ inch apart). Lay the fabric over them with web side against the wood. Cover the fabric with a thin towel, and use the iron to fuse the fabric to the wood. Next, place the piece of fabric facedown on a cutting board, and use a utility knife to cut around the wood shapes. Touch loose fabric with a dot of glue. Add embellishments like tiny wooden stars or buttons. Paint a name on either the fabric or wooden side. The back side can be left plain, painted, or fused with fabric. Lastly, use a tiny bit to drill a hole in the top of the ornament. Hang by gold thread or floss.

Elegant Crèche Ornament

1 Styrofoam ball
Paint
Short pins
Sequins
2 sizes of small beads

1 tiny plastic baby
2"x2" piece of white
    flannel
Heavy craft glue
Thread, string, or
    ribbon for a hanger

Hollow out a place in the middle of the foam ball. If so desired, paint the ball silver or gold. Starting with a small section, smooth on a thin layer of glue onto a pin, then one of the smallest beads, followed by the larger bead and a sequin. Stick the pin into the ball. Place beaded pins all around the ball, except for in the hollowed area. At the top, choose a place to anchor your hanger with a pin. In the area not covered by pins, spread a thin amount of glue, then sprinkle a generous amount of glitter to cover it. (Do this over a pan to catch the extra glitter.) Fold the flannel around the baby and secure with glue. Then glue the baby into the hollow of your ball. You can make a tiny bow to place at the top of the hollowed area.

Charming Ball Ornaments

Buy several clear glass ball ornaments. Each one can be made to look unique and special. Remove the metal hanger from the neck of the ball to reveal an opening. Decorate the inside, then replace the hanger.

BEACH BALL: Fill the ornament with tiny seashells and coral. Add a bit of sand.

FLOWER BALL: Take apart some colorful silk flowers and stuff them down the neck of the ornament. Cut a hole in a small doily and slip over the neck on the outside. Replace the hanger and tie a ribbon around it.

MARBLED PAINT BALL: Place a drop or two of paint inside the ornament and swirl it around to coat the inside, or try using a straw inserted into the neck of the ornament to blow the paint around. Use more than one color, either at the same time or with time in between for each color to dry. Paint should be thick enough to stick to the glass, but not so thick that it globs.

NATURE BALL: Fill $\frac{1}{3}$ of the ball with birdseed. Replace the hanger. Glue a little bit of artificial pine, a cinnamon stick branch, and a tiny mushroom bird to the neck of the ball.

PHOTO BALL: Cut a picture into a circle to fit the clear ball. Place the front inside against the glass. Stuff colored tinsel in behind the picture to hold it in place.

POPCORN BALL: Place 15–25 kernels of microwave popcorn (wiped clean of excess oils) inside the ball. Place the ornament in a paper bag and put in the microwave for 1–2 minutes (no metal). Listen carefully for the last pop; you may not need to leave the ornament in for the full time. When done popping, carefully remove the hot ornament. Sprinkle some glitter inside on the popcorn. Replace the hanger and tie a pretty ribbon around the neck.

POTPOURRI BALL: Use small pieces of potpourri to fill the ball. Hang it on your tree next to a light to warm up the potpourri and release the scent.

SAND ART BALL: Fill with layers of different colored sand.

WINTER SCENE BALL: Place very tiny pinecones in the ball and add artificial snowflakes.

Queen Anne's Lace Snowflakes

Several heads of Queen Anne's lace (a wildflower/weed found growing along roads, in fields, and in many backyards. The plants have big heads, which are clusters of tiny white flowers. They have a lacy look and 2–3' stalks.)

Spray snow

Clear acrylic spray paint

Thin gold cord

Hot glue and gun

This project could take 1–2 weeks to complete. First, cut the plant stalks a couple of inches below the heads. Gently rinse the heads under water (head facing down) and place on paper towel to dry. Trim the stem very close to the head. Lay heads on paper towels and carefully press flat.

Cover with more paper towel and place between heavy layers of paper as in phone books, newspapers, and catalogs. Check the flowers daily until they are just dry enough to hold the flat, lacy shape. Move them often so they don't stick to the paper. When the flowers are flat but still pliable, place them on a rack or screen and set them in an airy, though protected, place to dry for a day or two.

Make loops of the cord and glue to the back of each flower. Hang the flowers on a line outside or lay them on a protected surface. Spray them with snow. Apply several heavy coats, drying between. For the finishing touch spray generously with a coat of clear acrylic. A spray of glitter could also be applied.

Your snowflakes will require a gentle touch when handling.

Golden Stars

Piece of metal window screen
Gold spray paint

Gold fabric paint
Gold thread

Spray-paint the screen and let it dry. With a sharp permanent marker, draw or trace a star shape onto the screen. Cut out using old scissors. Squeeze fabric paint from the bottle onto the rough edge, creating a solid, raised line. Lay on waxed paper to dry. When dry, check that both sides of the edge have a solid line of paint. Apply more if needed. To the center, apply a design or write a word like "joy" or a name. Use gold thread to make a hanger.

Hanging Luminaries

Gather an assortment of small glass jelly, baby food, and other jars. Make sure that they have the ridge around the top for screwing on a lid. Use a medium gauge wire approximately 12–18 inches long. For each jar, twist one end around the jar, under the ridge. Make sure it is snug. Bend the remaining end straight up from the mouth of the jar and make a loop for a hanger. Add a ribbon tie around the jar's neck. Place a votive candle in each jar and fill the remaining space around the candle's bottom with rose hips. Hang an assortment of these luminaries from your porch railing or a variety of places where a candle can burn safely.

Stockings to Stuff

Use preprinted fabrics available for making stockings with instructions for assembly. Or you can take a piece of green or red felt and draw a stocking shape with a marker. Cut two matching pieces out with pinking shears. Place the pieces together and sew a $1/2$-inch seam around all but the top. If the stocking is large and will hold heavy items, go around with a second seam. You will have a rough edge around the stocking. Use ribbon, glue and glitter, rickrack, fabric paint, or other embellishments to dress up your creation. Attach a loop of cord to the top if you want to hang the stocking.

Popcorn Wreath

Cover a straw wreath with popcorn using hot glue. An average wreath will use two bags of microwave popcorn. Once the wreath is covered with the popcorn, spray-paint with gold or use a sponge to spot dab some gold highlights to the popcorn. Add a bow, some small greenery sprigs, and other frills to the top of the wreath.

Yo-Yo Wreath

Cut 8 circles (3 1/4 inches diameter) from green Christmas fabric. Cut 8 circles (1 1/2 inches diameter) from poster board. Leaving the thread unknotted with a long tail hanging out, make short running stitches around the circle of fabric folding 3/16 inch of the edge under as you go. Set your poster board circle in the center on the wrong side of the fabric, then pull the thread ends to gather the fabric circle. Tie the thread securely and trim the ends. Adjust the yo-yo so the hole is in the center. Glue a red or white button to the center hole of each yo-yo. Glue the yo-yos together by slightly overlapping the edges. Use a plastic lid or other circle as a guide as you shape the yo-yos into a circle. Glue a red bow to the top or bottom of the wreath. Make one stitch of thread through the back fabric of one yo-yo, and tie the ends in a loop for a hanger.

Metallic Wreath

Foam ring
Fake leaves removed from
   stems

Gold or silver spray
   paint
Hot glue

Spray-paint the foam and leaves separately. When dry, use hot glue to attach leaves to the wreath, overlapping edges. It is plain, but use your imagination and add embellishments as desired.

Fruit Candle Cups

Hollow out apples and oranges enough to fit a votive candle inside. Create a unique grouping on a platter with greenery and other fruits and nuts.

A Centerpiece That Grows

Cotton quilt batting
(avoid polyester)
1 dinner plate
1 tall, fat candle

$1/4$ c sproutable chive or
lentil seed (available
at a health food store)
Plastic wrap
Water spray bottle

Cover all but the center and outer edge of the plate with a layer of batting. Spray water over the batting. Scatter the seeds on and spray with more water. Carefully tip the plate to pour off any extra water. Tightly cover the plate with plastic wrap and put it in a well-lit place, but not in direct sunlight. Spray the batting every two days. When you see the first sprouts, remove the plastic wrap. Then spray with water daily. In 10–14 days, you should have a wreath of green sprouts. Place a candle in the center. The centerpiece will need to be kept in a sunlit place and watered regularly.

Holiday Potpourri

4 oranges
4 lemons
½ c whole cloves

½ c whole allspice
10 cinnamon sticks,
    broken
10 bay leaves, crumbled

Use a vegetable peeler to peel fruit carefully. Remove only the peel and not the white pith. Cut or tear peel into 1-inch pieces. Spread peel on a pan lined with a paper towel. Place in oven at 175° or on the oven's warm setting. Dry for 1½ hours, turning occasionally. Peels should be leathery and slightly brittle. Let stand and air dry on a paper towel for 24 hours. Combine with remaining ingredients. Keep in airtight container. To use: Let stand in a room in an open container or put 1 tablespoon of potpourri into 2 cups of hot water.

Dried Fruit

APPLES—Slice ⅛- to ¼-inch thick, including the core. Soak in lemon juice with salt for several minutes, then pat dry. They can also be sprinkled with a fruit preserver. You may want to sprinkle them with cinnamon for fragrance. Place on a lightly greased cookie sheet. Bake in a 150° oven for 6 hours. Slices should have a leathery texture. Spray with a few coats of clear acrylic.

ORANGES OR LEMONS—On a whole orange, use a knife or citrus peeler to cut approximately 6 lines down the sides and through the peel at intervals. Place on a cookie sheet and bake in a 150° oven for 10–12 hours. For slices, cut ⅛- to ¼-inch thick. Place on a lightly sprayed cookie sheet. Bake in a 150° oven for 6 hours or until edges start to curl and are pliable. Spray with a few coats of clear acrylic.

Use dried fruit on wreaths and garland, to enhance plain potpourri, or as an accent on almost anything like a gift, a picture frame, a tree ornament, and so on.

ADDITIONAL IDEA: Peel lemons and oranges, making sure to keep large sections of peel. Cut shapes in the peel with tiny cookie cutters. Allow them to air dry and add to your potpourri.

From the Kitchen

"Give, and it will be given to you.
A good measure, pressed down,
shaken together and running over,
will be poured into your lap."

LUKE 6:38

Chocolate-Dipped Spoons

Plastic spoons (find festive colors)
Chocolate chips (2 oz will do about 8 spoons)
Optional flavoring extracts (almond, peppermint, anise, etc.)

Melt chips over low heat until smooth. Dip spoons up to the start of the handle, allowing a good bit of chocolate to pool in the bowl. You can sprinkle with crushed candy canes while wet, or let the spoons dry on waxed paper and drizzle white chocolate over the dark chocolate. Try dipping half of the spoon in white chocolate and half in dark. Wrap dried spoons in plastic wrap and secure with ribbon. Use as stirrers in hot coffee, cappuccino, and cocoa.

Chocolate-Dipped Cookies

1 pkg sandwich cookies like Oreos or Nutter Butters (even home-
    made sugar cookies or chocolate chip cookies will work)
1 pkg white or chocolate almond bark
Edible sprinkle decorations (optional)

Melt almond bark in microwave or over low heat. When smooth and hot, carefully dip cookies, one at a time, into almond bark, covering $^1/_2$ to $^3/_4$ of cookie. Place on waxed paper and shake on sprinkles.

Chocolate-Dipped Candy Canes

Crushed, hard peppermint candy, red and green sprinkles,
or miniature chocolate chips (optional)

$\frac{1}{2}$ c semisweet chocolate chips or white vanilla chips	2 tsp shortening
	16 peppermint candy canes or sticks

Cover a cookie sheet with waxed paper. Melt chips and shortening in a saucepan over low heat until smooth. Dip $\frac{3}{4}$ of the candy cane in the chocolate. Lay on the waxed paper and allow it to cool about 2 minutes. Roll the chocolate-covered ends in decorative peppermint, sprinkles, or chips. Can be stored under loose cover for up to 2 weeks.

Peppermint Bark

16 oz of either vanilla-flavored baking chips or candy coating
24 hard peppermint candies

Line a large cookie sheet with waxed paper. Place peppermint candies in a heavy plastic bag and crush with a hammer or rolling pin. Slowly melt the chips over low heat, stirring constantly until smooth. Add crushed peppermints to melted chips. Spread mixture evenly out onto cookie sheet. Let stand in cool place for at least 1 hour. Break into pieces and store in an airtight container.

Cookie Suckers

When your cookies are ready to go into the oven, press an ice cream or lollipop stick into the dough, then bake. Cool completely. Wrap them individually with clear or colored plastic wrap, and tie the wrap in place with ribbon.

Candied Tea Stirrers

30–35 pieces of fruit-flavored hard candy, crushed
2 tablespoons light corn syrup
Sturdy plastic spoons

Line a cookie sheet with waxed paper and spray with cooking spray. Crush candies in a heavy plastic bag with a hammer or rolling pin. Add crushed candies to corn syrup and melt over low heat in a small saucepan. Stir often. Spoon candy into bowl of each plastic spoon. Place spoons on cookie sheet, allowing handles to rest on the raised sides so that the spoons are level. Let candy harden completely before storing in an air-tight container or wrapping with plastic wrap. Use the spoons to stir and add flavor to plain hot tea.

Hardtack Candy

1 c water
½ c light corn syrup
2 c sugar
Food coloring

½ tsp flavoring for candy making—orange or peppermint extract, cinnamon oil, or other

In a large, heavy saucepan, combine water, syrup, and sugar. Over medium heat, stir constantly until all is dissolved. Stop stirring and bring to 300° to 310°F (149° to 154°C) on a candy thermometer—or until a small amount of syrup dropped into cold water forms hard, brittle threads. Remove from heat and add flavoring and food coloring. Pour into a greased jelly roll pan and dust with powdered sugar. When cool, break into pieces. Store in airtight jars or bags.

Stuffed Sugar Dates

From Wanda Royer of Scio, OH

Box of whole dates
White granulated sugar

Walnut halves (broken in half)

Stuff each date with a piece of walnut. Roll the dates in a small bowl of sugar. Voila! Your treat is done.

Spiced Nuts

2 c whole almonds
2 c blanched peanuts
2 c sugar
½ c butter or margarine
3 tsp pumpkin pie spice

1 tsp allspice
1 tsp cinnamon
1 tsp ginger
1 tsp salt

Combine all ingredients in an electric skillet. Cook approximately 15 minutes over medium heat or at 350°, stirring and coating the nuts constantly until the sugar is melted and golden brown. Spread nuts in a thin layer onto a waxed paper or foil-lined cookie sheet to cool. Break into clusters.

Mocha Walnuts

½ c granulated sugar
½ c brown sugar,
   firmly packed
½ c sour cream
1 tbsp instant coffee

½ tsp ground cinnamon
¼ tsp ground nutmeg
1 tsp vanilla
3 c walnut halves

In a large saucepan, combine first 6 items, mixing well. Cook over medium heat, stirring constantly, to soft ball stage (238°). Remove from heat and stir in vanilla. Add nuts, stirring to coat. Spread onto a buttered baking sheet. Cool and break into pieces. Store in airtight container. Makes about 3½ cups nuts.

Crystallized Orange Pecans

1 c sugar
$\frac{1}{4}$ tsp ground cinnamon

$\frac{1}{4}$ c orange juice
2–3 c pecan halves

Combine all ingredients in $2\frac{1}{2}$-quart microwave-safe bowl. Cook uncovered on 70 percent power for 6 minutes (or medium power for 7–8 minutes). Stir, then resume cooking on 70 percent power for 8–10 minutes, or until crystallized, stirring several times. Spread nuts on waxed paper, avoid having them touch, and cool. Makes 2–3 cups.

Sticks and Stones Candy Mix

2 c pretzel sticks
4 c Cheerios cereal
4 c Corn Chex cereal
1 c salted peanuts

1–$1\frac{1}{2}$ lb white almond
    bark
1–2 tsp shortening
12-oz bag of M&Ms
    (or mixed nuts)

Melt bark with shortening over low heat. In a large bowl, combine pretzels, cereals, and nuts. Add half the melted bark to the mix and stir to coat. Add the other half and continue stirring until all is coated. Add M&Ms last and toss lightly (hot bark will cause them to melt). Spread on 2 to 3 waxed paper-lined cookie sheets. Refrigerate at least an hour. Break apart and store in an airtight container.

Almond Florentines

From Denise Hunter of Fort Wayne, IN

1 c butter (margarine will not suffice!)
1 c sugar
⅓ c honey
4 c sliced, blanched almonds

⅓ c whipping cream (heavy, sweet, liquid in a carton—not aerosol or freezer variety)
6 oz semisweet chocolate chips

Coat five 8-inch aluminum foil pie tins with cooking spray. Melt butter in your largest saucepan. Add sugar, honey, and cream. Bring to a boil over medium heat. Stir frequently. When the boil creates a wild froth on top, stir constantly and continue to boil at this level for exactly 90 seconds. Remove saucepan from heat. Add almonds; stir. Quickly pour mixture into the pie tins.

Bake 10–14 minutes until rich, golden brown (most likely will be bubbling). Cool in the pans for 20 minutes. Refrigerate in the pans for 30 minutes. Turn out onto waxed paper; stack in fridge with waxed paper in between. Melt chocolate and spread on the bottom of the Florentines. Let cool. Break into bark. Store in refrigerator with plastic wrap between layers.

Super Easy Fudge

⅔ c evaporated milk
(half of a regular can)
1⅔ c sugar
½ tsp salt
1½ c mini marshmallows
1 tsp vanilla

1½ c baking chips in your
choice of semisweet,
milk, or mint
chocolate, or peanut
butter
½ c nuts (optional)

Combine milk, sugar, and salt in a large saucepan over medium-low heat. Bring to a boil for 5 minutes, stirring constantly. Remove from heat. Add marshmallows, vanilla, and chips. Stir until smooth. Add nuts. Pour into a greased 9x9-inch pan. Refrigerate at least 1 hour until firm enough to cut. Store in an airtight container in a cool place.

Hot Fudge Sauce

12 oz can evaporated milk
12 oz semisweet
chocolate chips

1½ c white sugar
1 tsp butter
1 tsp vanilla

In a large saucepan, heat milk, chips, and sugar to boiling over medium heat, stirring constantly. Remove from heat. Stir in butter and vanilla. Serve warm over ice cream. Store tightly covered in refrigerator up to 4 weeks. Makes 3 cups.

Easy Apple Butter

5 ½ lb apples, peeled
    and finely chopped
4 c sugar

¼ tsp ground cloves
¼ tsp salt
3 tsp cinnamon

Place apples in a Crock-Pot. Combine sugar, cloves, salt, and cinnamon. Pour the seasoning over the apples and mix well. Cover and cook on high for 1 hour. Reduce heat to low; cook for 9–11 hours or until the mixture thickens and is dark brown, stirring occasionally (stir more frequently as it thickens to prevent sticking). Uncover and cook on low 1 hour longer. If desired, stir with a wire whisk until smooth. Spoon into freezer containers, leaving ½ inch headspace. Cover and refrigerate, or freeze, or can in hot water bath. Enjoy the fragrance in the house as this cooks!

Butter Blends

1 c (2 sticks) of butter or margarine, softened

Beat with one of the following groups of ingredients:

HERB: $\frac{1}{4}$ to $\frac{1}{2}$ cup chopped fresh or 1 to 2 tablespoons dried herb (basil, chives, oregano, savory, tarragon, or thyme), 1 tablespoon lemon juice, and $\frac{1}{4}$ teaspoon salt

GARLIC: 2 teaspoons paprika, $\frac{1}{2}$ teaspoon pepper, and 8 cloves crushed garlic

ALMOND: 2 tablespoons finely chopped almonds and 1 teaspoon almond extract

RASPBERRY: 1 cup crushed raspberries and 2 tablespoons sugar or $\frac{1}{2}$ cup raspberry jam

ORANGE: 2 teaspoons grated orange peel and 2 tablespoons orange juice

Refrigerate in tightly covered container up to 3 weeks or freeze up to 2 months. Delicious with breads, even with vegetables and meats.

Herb Shake

2 tsp garlic powder
2 tsp onion powder
2 tsp paprika
2 tsp white pepper

2 tsp dry mustard
1 tsp powdered thyme
1 tsp ground celery
   seed

Blend the herbs and store in a shaker. Great way to add taste to salads, meat, poultry, and vegetables.

Homemade Herb Vinegar

2 c white wine vinegar
$\frac{1}{2}$ c firmly packed fresh herb (basil, chives, dill weed, mint, oregano, rosemary, or tarragon)

Shake vinegar and the herb of your choice in a sealed glass jar. Allow to stand in a cool, dry place for 10 days. Strain the vinegar. Place 1 sprig of fresh herb of the same variety in a decorative jar or bottle and add strained vinegar.

Can substitute these for the herb: 6 cloves of garlic or $\frac{1}{2}$ cup chopped peeled gingerroot.

Homemade Fruit Vinegar

3 c white wine vinegar   2 tbsp honey
2 c of crushed berry like raspberry, blueberry, or cranberry
     (frozen or fresh) or ¼ c lemon or orange rind, shredded

Combine in large saucepan and cover. Bring to a boil, then remove from heat and let stand until cooled. Strain the fruit or rind out. Pour into bottle(s) and seal tightly. Allow to stand at least 24 hours before adding some decorative fruit or rind to the vinegar. Seal tightly. Store at room temperature. Good for approximately 3 months.

Vinegars can be used on salads and vegetables or as marinade for meat, poultry, or fish. The bottles are pretty given unwrapped, just add a touch of ribbon or raffia to the neck.

Homemade Oil

1 c walnuts, almonds, or hazelnuts   2 c vegetable oil

Combine nuts and ½ cup oil in blender until nuts are finely chopped. Put nut mixture and remaining oil in a glass container. Cover tightly and allow to stand in a cool, dry place for 10 days. Strain the oil. Store in the refrigerator in a sealed glass bottle. Lasts up to 3 months. Use to accent salads and meats.

Frozen Cookie Dough

This year give those short on time (or skill) a gift of cookie dough to bake on those cold, lazy winter evenings after the holiday goodies are gone. Plan to give each person a variety of dough. Use basic recipes for chocolate chip, oatmeal, and peanut butter cookies. Mix up double batches. Put straight into freezer-safe plastic containers or bags. Or, so only what is needed can be baked instead of the whole batch, form the dough into balls and freeze on a cookie sheet. When frozen put them into bags and store in the freezer. Dough will last longer in the freezer than baked cookies, and the recipient will be able to enjoy the cookies warm from the oven. When you give the dough, include a note with baking instructions.

Jar Cakes

Bake a cake in a sterilized, 12-ounce, wide-mouth canning jar. Any quick bread recipe will work, and one recipe stretches over approximately 6 jars. The cake should not bake and rise to more than $^1/_4$ to $^1/_2$ inch from the jar lip. Wipe any drips from the sides. Bake one jar alone first, and gauge how much batter is right. Also gauge appropriate baking time as it can vary as much as 25 to 40 minutes. Record the figures on your recipe for the future. If you have multiple jars in the oven, move the jars during the baking process to encourage even baking. Use heavy mitts to handle the hot jars. Cover with new, boil-prepared lid and ring seal while cake is still hot. The heat should seal them. May store in a cool, dark place up to 3 months. The bread is safe to use as long as the vacuum seal holds and no mold growth appears. The jar cakes serve 1 to 2 people and remain very moist.

Brownie Jar Cake

2 sterilized 12-oz canning jars
1 c flour
1 c sugar
$\frac{1}{2}$ tsp baking soda
$\frac{1}{4}$ tsp cinnamon
   (optional)
$\frac{1}{3}$ c butter or margarine

$\frac{1}{4}$ c water
3 tbsp cocoa
$\frac{1}{4}$ c buttermilk
1 egg, beaten
$\frac{1}{2}$ tsp vanilla
$\frac{1}{4}$ c walnuts, finely
   chopped

Brush melted shortening on the inside walls of sterilized jars. (Do not spray with oil or use butter.) In a small bowl, blend flour, sugar, baking soda, and cinnamon. Set aside. In a medium saucepan, combine butter, water, and cocoa. Heat over low and stir until butter melts and mixture is well blended. Remove from heat and stir in the dry mixture. Add buttermilk, egg, and vanilla. Beat by hand until smooth. Fold in nuts. Pour equally into prepared jars. Place jars on a cookie sheet in 325° oven for 35–40 minutes or until a pick inserted deep into the cake comes out clean. Remove from the oven and immediately place a hot lid onto the jars and hold snug with a ring.

Pumpkin Spice Jar Cake

8 sterilized 12-oz
   canning jars
1 c raisins, coarsely chopped
1 c walnuts, coarsely chopped
2 c flour
2 tsp baking soda
$\frac{1}{4}$ tsp baking powder
$\frac{1}{2}$ tsp salt

2 tsp ground cloves
2 tsp cinnamon
1 tsp ginger
4 large eggs
2 c sugar
1 c oil
16 oz pumpkin (not pie
   filling)

Sterilize jars and, when cooled, brush melted shortening on the inside walls. (Do not spray with oil or use butter.) Combine raisins and walnuts; set aside. Sift dry ingredients together in a large bowl. Add raisins and walnuts; set aside. In another large bowl, beat eggs at high speed 2–3 minutes until thick and yellow. Gradually beat in sugar until thick and light in color. At low speed, beat in oil and pumpkin until well blended. Divide batter among the 8 jars (should be slightly less than half full). Place jars on a cookie sheet in 325° oven for 35–40 minutes or until a pick inserted deep into the cake comes out clean. Remove from the oven and immediately place a hot lid onto the jars and hold snug with a ring.

Gingerbread Jar Cake

5 sterilized 12-oz canning jars
2 $\frac{1}{4}$ c flour
$\frac{3}{4}$ c sugar
1 tsp baking soda
$\frac{1}{2}$ tsp baking powder
$\frac{1}{4}$ tsp salt

2 tsp ginger
1 tsp cinnamon
$\frac{1}{2}$ tsp ground cloves
$\frac{3}{4}$ c margarine, softened
$\frac{3}{4}$ c water
$\frac{1}{2}$ c molasses

Brush melted shortening on the inside walls of sterilized jars. (Do not spray with oil or use butter.) In a large bowl, combine dry ingredients. Stir in margarine, water, and molasses. Divide batter equally among the 5 jars (they should be about half full). Place jars on a cookie sheet in 325° oven for 35–40 minutes or until a pick inserted deep into the cake comes out clean. Remove from the oven and immediately place a hot lid onto the jars and hold snug with a ring.

Cobbler Mix in a Jar

1 c all-purpose flour
1 tsp baking powder

1 c sugar
1 tsp powdered vanilla

Combine and blend the ingredients in a small bowl. Store in an air-tight container.

INSTRUCTION CARD:
Serves 8 to 10

4 c fresh or frozen berries
    (blueberries, raspberries, or
    blackberries)
¼ c orange juice
¼ c sugar

1 tsp cinnamon
1 c butter, melted
1 egg
1 jar cobbler mix

Preheat oven to 375°. In large mixing bowl, combine berries, juice, sugar, and cinnamon. Place berries in a 9x13-inch pan. In small mixing bowl, blend the butter with the egg. Add the cobbler mix and stir until the mixture sticks together. Drop the dough by tablespoonfuls on top of the berry filling. Bake for 35–45 minutes or until the topping is golden brown and the filling is bubbling. Allow to cool for 15 minutes before serving.

Blonde Brownie Mix in a Jar

2 c brown sugar
2 c all-purpose flour

½ c chopped pecans

Combine ingredients. Store in a jar or heavy plastic bag.

INSTRUCTION CARD:
Combine mix with 4 eggs and blend well. Pour into a greased 9x13-inch pan. Bake at 350° for 25–28 minutes.

Fudge Brownie Mix in Jar

2 c sugar
1 c cocoa (not Dutch
  process)

1 c all-purpose flour
1 c chopped pecans
1 c chocolate chips

Mix all the ingredients together and store in an airtight container.

INSTRUCTION CARD:
Makes 24

1 c butter or margarine,
  softened

4 eggs
1 jar fudge brownie mix

Preheat the oven to 325°. Grease a 9x13-inch pan. In a large bowl, cream the butter with a mixer. Add the eggs, one at a time, beating well. Add the brownie mix and continue to beat the mixture until it is smooth. Spread into the greased pan and bake for 40–50 minutes.

Candy Cookie Mix in a Jar

½ c sugar
½ c brown sugar,
    firmly packed

1 tsp powdered vanilla
1 tsp baking soda
2 c flour

Combine all ingredients in a medium bowl. Whisk the ingredients together until they are evenly distributed, making sure all brown sugar lumps are crushed. Store in an airtight jar.

INSTRUCTION CARD:
Makes 3 dozen cookies

1 c unsalted butter or
    margarine, softened

1 large egg
1 jar candy cookie mix

1 c candy bar chunks (Reese's peanut butter cups,
    Butterfinger bars, white or milk chocolate chunks)

Preheat oven to 350°. In a large bowl, beat the butter with a mixer until it is smooth. Add the egg, and continue beating until the egg is well blended. Add the cookie mix and candy bar chunks and blend on low. Form the cookies into 1½-inch balls and place them 2 inches apart on an ungreased cookie sheet. Bake for 10–12 minutes, until golden on the edges. Remove from oven and cool on cookie sheet for 2 minutes.

Magic Cookie Bar Mix in a Jar

$^1/_4$ c walnuts, chopped
1 c butterscotch chips
1 c semisweet
   chocolate chips

$^1/_2$ c shredded coconut
1 c graham crackers,
   crushed

Combine ingredients in a wide-mouth glass canning jar by order listed above.

INSTRUCTION CARD:

Preheat oven to 350°. Add $^1/_2$ cup melted butter to graham crackers. Place in a 9x9-inch baking pan and pat to evenly cover the bottom. Scatter remaining ingredients on top. Pour a 14-ounce can of sweetened condensed milk evenly over everything. Bake for 30 minutes.

Snickerdoodle Mix in a Jar

2¾ cups all-purpose flour
¼ tsp salt
1 tsp baking soda

2 tsp cream of tartar
1½ c sugar

In a large bowl, combine the ingredients with a whisk. Store the mix in an airtight container.

INSTRUCTION CARD:
Makes about 5 dozen cookies

1 c butter or margarine,
    softened
2 eggs

1 jar Snickerdoodle mix
½ c sugar
1 tbsp cinnamon

Preheat oven to 350°. In a large bowl, use an electric mixer to cream the butter until fluffy. Add the eggs and beat on low speed until the mixture is smooth. Add the mix and continue to beat on low speed until the dough begins to form. Shape the dough into 1-inch balls and roll in a blend of the cinnamon and sugar. Arrange on ungreased baking sheets 2 inches apart and bake for 16–19 minutes, or until light tan. Place on wire racks to cool.

Peach Tea Mix

1 c instant tea mix   2 c granulated sugar
1 box peach gelatin

Combine all ingredients in a large bowl; mix well. Store in an airtight container. To serve, stir about 2 teaspoons of tea mix into 8 ounces of hot water.

Friendship Tea

2 c orange drink mix   ¼ oz package of
2 c sugar   lemonade powder
¾ c instant tea mix   1½ tsp cinnamon
¾ tsp ground cloves

Combine all ingredients and store in airtight container. To brew: Add 3–4 teaspoons tea mix to 1 cup boiling water. Stir until mix completely dissolves.

Friendship Soup Mix in a Jar

$\frac{1}{2}$ c dry split peas
$\frac{1}{3}$ c beef bouillon
  (low sodium)
$\frac{1}{4}$ c pearl barley
$\frac{1}{2}$ c dry lentils

$\frac{1}{4}$ c dried minced onion
2 tsp Italian seasoning
$\frac{1}{2}$ c uncooked long grain
  brown rice
$\frac{1}{2}$ c alphabet macaroni

In a $1\frac{1}{2}$-pint or 1-quart jar, layer the eight ingredients in the order listed. Seal tightly. (If ingredients do not come right up to the top of the jar, you can place a crumpled piece of plastic wrap on top of the last layer to keep layers from shifting.) Store in a cool, dry place until ready to use.

INSTRUCTION CARD:

To prepare soup, you'll need one pound of lean ground beef and a 28-ounce can of diced tomatoes. Remove macaroni from top of jar and set aside. In a large saucepan or Dutch oven, brown beef and drain. Add 3 quarts of water, tomatoes with juice, and soup mix, then bring to a boil. Reduce heat and cover. Simmer for 45 minutes. Add the reserved macaroni and cover. Simmer for 15–20 minutes or until macaroni, peas, lentils, and barley are tender. Yield: 1 batch serves 16.

Spicy Chili Seasoning Mix in a Jar

4 tbsp chili powder
2½ tsp ground coriander
2½ tsp ground cumin

1½ tsp garlic powder
1 tsp dried oregano
½ tsp cayenne pepper

Mix the above and place in a jelly jar. Makes 20 teaspoons of mix or 6 batches of chili.

INSTRUCTION CARD:

Brown 2 pounds lean ground beef and 1 medium chopped onion. Blend in 3 teaspoons chili seasoning. Add a 28-ounce can of tomatoes and two 15-ounce cans of chili beans. Simmer 40–50 minutes.

Mexican Dip Mix in a Jar

½ c dried parsley
⅓ c dried minced onion
¼ c dried chives

⅓ c chili powder
¼ c ground cumin
¼ c salt

In a large bowl, combine the spices and store in an airtight container.
This dip mix can be given in a small sombrero.

INSTRUCTION CARD:

3 tbsp dip mix
1 c mayonnaise (may use
low-fat)

1 c sour cream or low-fat
plain yogurt

In a medium mixing bowl combine ingredients. Whisk the mixture
until smooth. Refrigerate for 2–4 hours. Serve with tortilla chips or
fresh vegetables. Makes 2 cups.

Dog Biscuit Mix in a Jar

1 c all-purpose unbleached
  flour
1 c whole wheat flour
½ c yellow cornmeal
½ tsp garlic powder

½ c instant nonfat dry
  milk powder
1 tsp brown sugar or
  white sugar
Pinch of salt

In a medium mixing bowl, combine all ingredients. Pour into a 1-quart, wide-mouth canning jar. Close jar tightly. Tie a dog biscuit cookie cutter and instruction card around the top of the jar with a pretty ribbon.

INSTRUCTION CARD:

Position a rack in the center of the oven. Preheat to 250°. Place contents of the jar in a medium-sized bowl. Add one large egg, ½ cup shredded sharp cheddar cheese, ¼ cup grated Parmesan cheese, ¼ to ½ cup hot chicken broth, beef broth, or very hot water.

Make very heavy, but not sticky, dough. Add more flour or water, a spoonful at a time if dough is too moist (use flour) or too dry (use hot water).

Turn out dough onto a floured pastry cloth and knead 8–10 times until elastic. Let dough rest for 5 minutes. Roll out dough ½-inch thick and cut with a dog-bone shaped cutter. Place cookies close together. They will not spread.

Bake for 1 hour, rotate the baking trays in the oven (turn tray around 180 degrees), and bake them another half hour. Cool the cookies in the pan for 1 minute, then transfer to a wire cake rack to cool completely.

Gift Bundles

*Each man should give what
he has decided in his heart to give,
not reluctantly or under compulsion,
for God loves a cheerful giver.*

2 CORINTHIANS 9:7

*F*ill an inexpensive basket or other container with a variety of items that will be meaningful to a special person.

FOR TEA TIME: A teacup. A teapot. Strainer. A variety of teas. A small jar of honey. Homemade jams or jellies with crackers or a small loaf of homemade bread. Shortbread cookies. Tea stirrers.

FOR BATH TIME: Bath salts. Scented soaps and lotions. Sponge. Scented candle. Washcloths. Chocolate truffles. A doorknob sign that says "Pampering. Do Not Disturb."

FOR FAMILY NIGHT: A family-friendly movie on VHS or DVD or a gift certificate to a video rental store. Two bags of microwave popcorn. Theater-sized boxes of candy. Kool-Aid mix in envelopes or 4 cans of soda pop.

FOR THE GARDENER: Small hand tools (spade, trowel, rake, and cutters). Gloves. Knee pads. Plant markers. Seed packets. Bulbs. Bonemeal or other multipurpose fertilizer. (Place things in a bucket or watering can.)

FOR THE BIRDWATCHER: Bird feeder. A bag of birdseed. Suet with cage. Bird guidebook. Rain gauge. Outdoor thermometer.

FOR THE DO-IT-YOURSELF PERSON: Tape measure. Hammer. Screwdriver with changeable heads. Variety box of nails and screws. Small level. Tool apron. Utility knife. Safety glasses. Superglue. Duct tape. How-to book.

FOR THE WRITER: Stationery. Pens. Envelopes. Stamps. Postcards. Address book (with some special addresses already included).

FOR THE TEACHER: Colorful pencils. Erasers. Post-it notepads. Packets of stickers. Red pens. Highlighters.

FOR THE STUDENT: Calculator. Notebooks. Pencils, pens, and highlighters. Study lamp. Dictionary and thesaurus. Post-it notepads in various sizes.

FOR THE NEW MOM: A large bottle of pain reliever. Hand lotion. A picture frame. A brag book. A CD of favorite lullabies. Chocolate. Coffee. Coupons promising your babysitting services.

FOR THE BABY: A boo-boo bunny. First Christmas ornament. Containers of powder, baby lotion, baby wash or
shampoo, diaper rash ointment, and baby wipes.
Washcloths. Burping cloths. Receiving blankets. A
teething ring. Pacifier. Bib. Night-light. (Place in a
diaper bag or small waste can.)

FOR THE COOK: Measuring spoons and cups. Spices.
Apron. Kitchen timer. Recipe box or other organizer.
Cookbook. Small mixing bowls. Whisk. Box of storage
bags. (Use a large mixing bowl or colander lined with a
dish towel to hold things.)

FOR THE OUTDOOR CHEF: Barbecue tools. Aluminum
foil. Lighter fluid. Apron. Citronella candles. Bug
spray. (Place everything in a cooler.)

FOR THE BOOK LOVER: Two or three new books. Small
reading lamp. Bookmark. Packets of coffee or tea.
Cookies.

FOR THE CHOCOLATE LOVER: A package of candy
bars. Brownies with fudge icing. Truffles. German

chocolate cake. Several variations of fudge. Chocolate syrup. A couple packages of chocolate pudding mix. Chocolate-covered pretzels. Chocolate/fudge butter cookies. Hot chocolate mix.

FOR THE CAR LOVER: A steering wheel cover. An ice scraper. A sun shade. A fire extinguisher. Some silly fuzzy dice. An air freshener. A bottle of car wash, tire cleaner, spot remover, and car wax. A buffer cloth. (Use a bucket to hold everything.)

FOR THE SPORTS LOVER: A sports blunders video. Small game balls. A pack of trading cards. Ball cap.

FOR THE COFFEE LOVER: A special coffee cup. A variety of small packets of flavored coffee. Small jar of creamer (also available in flavors). Bean grinder. Chocolate-dipped cinnamon sticks or spoons. Butter cookies.

FOR THE PET LOVER: A ball. Squeak toys. Chews. Treats. Book on pet care. Collar, leash, and name tag. Bowl with pet's name on it.

The Wrap Up

*"The Lord Jesus himself said:
'It is more blessed to give than to
receive.'"*

ACTS 20:35

Design Your Own Gift Wrap!

Be creative by combining and designing with the following:

Brown packing paper or
white butcher paper or
even large brown paper
grocery bags
Rubber stamps and ink
Stickers

Paint
Design tools (sponge,
cotton balls, toothbrush,
old pot scrubber, straw
to blow paint)

Alternative Papers

Who says you have to use only Christmas-printed papers?

- Try using leftover wallpaper or shelf paper.
- Paper with your child's drawings from school, old maps, news-
  paper, and the comics.
- Wrap a box with plain paper and glue old Christmas cards to
  the sides.
- Even aluminum foil and colored plastic wrap will work.

Reusable Wraps

As an alternative to store-bought paper that can get expensive, try wrapping a box in something that can be reused by the recipient.

Bandana or scarf
Blanket
Fabric
Laundry bag

Pillowcase
Tablecloth
Towel
Tulle, netting, or lace

Window Box

Cut one or more designs in the lid of a shoebox, copier paper box, or other box with solid lid. Wrap the box with paper, trimming flush with the cutout. Tape plastic wrap (clear or colored) over the cutout on the inside of the box. Let your gift peek through.

Window Bag

Cut a design out on one side of a sturdy bag. Cover the cutout on the inside with clear or colored plastic wrap. Fill the bag, then fold the top over, letting a hint of the contents show through. With a hole punch, put two holes at least 1 inch apart in the top fold. Put ribbon, raffia, or yarn through the holes and tie a bow that hangs above the window.

Fabric Gift Bags

Cut a 16x19-inch rectangle of holiday fabric for each bag. Lay a 2-foot piece of narrow cord or ribbon along the 19-inch side and turn 1 inch of fabric over the cord, wrong sides facing. Stitch $\frac{1}{4}$ inch from the edge. Fold the 16-inch sides together with right sides facing. Stitch a $\frac{1}{2}$-inch seam around the 3 rough sides. Trim the corners, and turn right side out.

SHORTCUT:
Cut 2 pieces of calico, flannel, or felt with pinking shears to 9x12 inches. With wrong sides facing, sew $\frac{1}{2}$-inch seam. (You could hand-sew it with embroidery floss.) Fill the bag with a small gift, gather the top closed, and secure with a ribbon or raffia bow.

Fabric Envelopes

To make a fabric envelope that will measure 5x8 inches, cut a piece of holiday fabric 8x13 inches with pinking shears. Measure 3 inches up the long side and mark it with a pin (you'll have a 3-inch flap). Fold the 8-inch end up to the pin (wrong sides facing) so that your pouch area will be 5 inches deep. Sew a $\frac{1}{2}$-inch seam around the 3 sides of the pouch area; $\frac{3}{4}$-inch from the unsewn edge of the flap, cut a small slit in the center of the flap. Lay the flap over the pouch and mark where the slit touches the pouch. Fold a 6- to 8-inch piece of $\frac{1}{4}$-inch ribbon in half, and at the fold, hand-sew it onto the pouch at the mark. Fill your pouch with the gift, fold flap over, and secure with ribbon.

Tag It

- Print free gift tag designs from the Internet.
- Print your own tag design onto a sheet of computer labels.
- Simply fold a rectangular piece of matching wrapping paper in half for a little card tag.
- Use a bookmark or other card with sentiment that you can write the name on.
- Buy a key chain, ink pen, magnet, jewelry pin, or other item with the recipient's name preprinted on it.

Ornament Tags

Buy inexpensive, plain-colored ornaments with matte finish. Use a pointed, permanent marker to write the recipient's name.

Shipping Cookies

Bar cookies and drop cookies like plain chocolate chip and peanut butter travel best. Frosted and filled cookies may soften and stick together. Cool cookies completely before packing. Carefully pack the cookies between layers of waxed paper in a tin, empty coffee can, or rigid box. Pack a piece of apple or slice of bread with soft cookies to keep them fresh. Use crumpled waxed paper or plain popcorn to fill in any open space. There should be no room for the cookies to shift. Pack this tin in a larger, sturdy shipping box. Pad the area around the tin with crumpled paper or other packing material, seal, and address. Write "perishable" on the box.

101 *Tree-*
TRIMMING
IDEAS

*T*he evergreen tree strung with lights and colored balls often stands at the heart of our homes' Christmas decorations. When the tree is up, we know Christmas is really here.

Although the Christmas tree tradition has its roots in many pagan celebrations, it is also a truly Christian symbol, as well. In fact, Martin Luther, the great Protestant reformer, is credited with starting the custom of decorating trees for Christmas. Walking home one clear winter night, he is said to have looked up and seen stars shining through the branches of an evergreen tree. The scene was so lovely that he recreated it by bringing a tree into his home and fastening candles to its branches. "Christ's tree," he called it, a symbol of our evergreen life in Jesus—He who is the Light of the world.

Starchy String Ornaments

MATERIALS

thick cotton string
liquid starch

colored cellophane
white glue

Place string in liquid starch to soak. Arrange in desired shapes on top of colored cellophane and, using white glue, drizzle all around each shape; lay another sheet of cellophane on top and allow to dry. Cut out around the outside of the string shapes; punch holes through tops and string to hang from chandelier, in front of windows, or on the tree.

Angel Ornaments

MATERIALS

white poster paint
stiff blue paper
markers
white glue

glitter glue
clear contact paper
gold cord

Have children dip their hands in white poster paint and transfer prints to blue paper in a fan pattern. Let dry and cut out to create angel wings. Cut out an angel head (circular shape) and body (triangular shape) from additional paper, and glue wings and head to body. Children may draw details of face, hair, and angel gowns. Add glitter to a sparkly halo. Place completed angel between two sheets of clear contact paper and cut around outer edge to laminate. Punch a hole in the top and hang with gold cord.

And, lo,
the angel of the Lord came upon them,
and the glory of the Lord shone round about them. . . .
And the angel said unto them,
Fear not: for, behold,
I bring you good tidings of great joy.

LUKE 2:9–10 KJV

Angels, from the realms of glory,
Wing your flight o'er all the earth;
Ye who sang creation's story,
Now proclaim the Messiah's birth:
Come and worship. Come and worship.
Worship Christ, the newborn King!

JAMES MONTGOMERY

Pom-Pom Wreaths for the Tree

Materials

white glue
package of green pom-poms
wooden drapery ring
red embroidery floss (or string)

package of tiny red
pom-poms
narrow ribbon

Glue green pom-poms one by one onto drapery ring until completely covered and ring looks like a wreath. Glue a few tiny red pom-poms onto wreath for berries. Let dry. Pull a festive patterned ribbon through the hook on the ring and tie. Hang from embroidery floss pulled through the hook.

Golden Lamé Ornaments

MATERIALS

½ yard gold lamé
½ yard white
   polyester backing

cotton and metallic
   threads
small bag of polyester
   stuffing

Draw simple star and crescent moon patterns on paper, about 3 inches across. Fold fabric in half with right sides together; pin on patterns and trace outlines with a pencil. Cut through both layers adding a ¼-inch seam allowance. Baste along penciled outline leaving a 1½-inch hole for stuffing. Machine-stitch using ¼-inch seams and clip seams at angles of star arms and at ¼-inch intervals on concave curve of moon. Turn shapes right side out and fill with polyester filling. Hand-stitch opening closed and run metallic thread through tip of each ornament for hanging.

Sparkling Prisms to Light Your Tree

MATERIALS

chandelier prisms (available at home center stores)

wire ornament hangers

12-inch pieces of ribbon

Simply attach an ornament hanger to the top of the prism and tie a dainty bow (something Victorian and lacy looks nice) at the top, allowing the ribbon ends to trail down the sides of the prism. This technique can also be used to create unique ornaments using old pieces of cast-off jewelry.

Lacy Heart Tree Ornaments

MATERIALS

candy cane
2½-yard piece of 4-inch-wide ruffled lace

glue gun
small silk rose
thin piece of ribbon

Sew a casing in lace starting half an inch from plain edge. Cut lace in half and insert candy cane into each piece, gathering ruffle as you go. Attach candy canes at bottom and top with glue gun to form a heart. When dry, attach silk rose at center point with glue and affix ribbon loop at back for hanging.

In him was life;
and the life was the light of men.
And the light shineth in darkness;
and the darkness comprehended it not. . . .
That was the true Light,
which lighteth every man
that cometh into the world.

JOHN 1:4–5, 9 KJV

Ribbon Tree

(an alternative to an evergreen tree)

MATERIALS

5-inch Styrofoam ball
12-inch wooden dowel or
    squared wood trim, for stem
basket
ready-to-mix cement

selection of ribbons in
    different colors and
    widths, about 6½ yards
    of each
florist's spool wire
reindeer moss

Spear the Styrofoam ball on the dowel. Mix enough cement to almost fill the lined basket and pour in. Place dowel in center of basket and secure with a web of masking tape across the top of pot. Let dry for 24 hours. Cut ribbon in strips 7 inches long. Double up ribbon to form single-loop bows and twist wire around center, leaving one long end to stud ball completely with bows. Spread reindeer moss out over base of tree.

Jingle Bell Tree

MATERIALS

lightweight wire
wire cutters
red berry cluster
sprigs of evergreen

large gold jingle bell
(available at craft
and fabric stores)
1¼ yards of 2-inch–
wide sheer ribbon

Wire berry cluster and evergreen together; run wire through hanging loop of jingle bell. Thread ribbon through hanging loop and tie a bow in ribbon about 7 inches above the ornament.

Jingle bells, jingle bells,
Jingle all the way!
O what fun it is to ride
In a one-horse open sleigh!

TRADITIONAL

Mobiles for the Tree

Create a variety of mobiles for the little ones in the family using mobile wires (available at craft stores), monofilament thread, and any of the following:

MATERIALS

cutout greeting cards	tree ornaments
toy airplanes	tiny stuffed animals
angels	

Or use leftover scraps of fabric to cut out little figures or other Christmas shapes to sew and stuff—anything with bright colors and prints to stimulate baby's eyes. The important thing to remember in composing a mobile is maintaining balance. Begin hanging dangling things from top wires using thread. Adjust lengths of string to balance each side and work downward, adding new wires and hooks to keep in balance. Don't crowd objects together.

Patriotic Tree

Decorate a tree with miniature variations of the American flag reflecting different periods of our nation's history. Include any other ornaments that fit with this theme such as stars, eagles, toy soldiers, drums, etc.

Wire Treetop Star

To make this star, simply shape and twist lengths of 12-gauge and 26-gauge wire. Make the basic form with the larger wire and wind the smaller wire across the completed form for a bright and shiny treetop ornament.

When they saw the star,
they rejoiced with exceeding great joy.

MATTHEW 2:10 KJV

Star of wonder, star of night,
Star with royal beauty bright;
Westward leading, still proceeding,
Guide us to thy perfect light!

JOHN HENRY HOPKINS, JR.

Spiky Christmas Stars

Cut a circle 6 inches in diameter from silver or gold foil. Mark off 8 equal sections, being careful not to draw a line to the center of the circle. Leave a circle about $1^1/_2$ inches in diameter in the center. Cut along each of the fold lines. With the tip of a sharp pencil, start folding the edges of each cut section in a clockwise fashion. Continue rolling each section until the piece takes on the shape of a cone. Cut several more of these circles following these steps. Put one layer on top of the first so that the points of one circle fall in the open spaces of the layer below. Continue placing each layer upon layer, gluing the centers together until you have formed a half ball. The more layers you place on top of one another, the fuller the ornament will appear. Then make a second half ball and glue both halves together. Hang from the tree with transparent thread.

Ribbon Candy Ornaments

With a needle and metallic thread, run through a length of colorful ribbon at regular intervals. Draw up to create ribbon candy effect, knot, and create loop for tree hanger.

Peppermint Stick Icicles

Wrap strips of silver paper and red ribbon together around cyclinder-shaped object to create spirals. Sew silver thread through top of "candy cane" or "icicle," tie thread around artificial holiday greenery and berries, and hang it from tree.

Checkerboard Quilt Ornaments

Cut slits in paper squares and weave bits of ribbon in and out using different color combinations for quilt effect. Outline and hang "quilt" with bric-a-brac.

Snowman Tree

Have your children each make little paper snowmen to represent themselves, printing their names across the bottom, and pasting twigs on trunk for arms. Wrap with gaily colored ribbon for scarf. Paste longer twig to bottom of snowmen and anchor in a basket of pinecones to create the tree. This might be a nice gift for a family of cousins to create for grandparents with tiny school pictures cut out and pasted on the head of each snowman.

Snowball Ornament

MATERIALS

12-gauge wire
wire cutters
plastic foam balls in assorted
    sizes
needle-nose pliers

plaster mix
old spoon
pearlescent white
    spray paint
white glitter

Cut a length of wire and insert it almost all the way through a foam ball. Using pliers, twist the wire into a curlicue or curl it around a pencil to form a spiral. Mix the plaster according to manufacturer's directions until it's the consistency of thick frosting. Dip the ball in plaster; use a spoon to spread the plaster evenly over the ball. Hang the ball to dry, suspending it on a string stretched between two chairs, spreading newspaper below to catch drips. Allow 24 hours to dry, then spray with paint, sprinkle with glitter, and dry. Attach to a bow and add clusters of berries for color.

Purge me with hyssop,
and I shall be clean:
wash me,
and I shall be whiter than snow.

PSALM 51:7 KJV

Come now, and let us reason together. . .
though your sins be as scarlet,
they shall be as white as snow.

ISAIAH 1:18 KJV

Paradise Trees

Another source for the Christmas tree tradition can be traced back to the medieval miracle plays performed during the fourteenth and fifteenth centuries on the twenty-fourth of December. Since few people could read in medieval times, miracle plays acted out stories from the Bible. In the early church calendar of saints, December 24 was Adam and Eve's Day, so the dramatic events of the fruit tree and the Garden of Eden were depicted. Before the performance, the actors would often parade through the streets, and "Adam" would carry the "paradise tree," which was usually an evergreen tree decorated with apples. This was the only prop on stage during the play, so long after the miracle plays were no longer performed, it was connected in people's minds with Christmas.

Paradise Tree Decorations

The paradise tree was hung with apples, cherries, and white wafers or cookies. The apples symbolized the forbidden fruit and the fall of humankind, while the white wafers represented the communion bread, symbolic of humanity's salvation through Jesus Christ. Their presence on the same tree showed that even though humanity was sinful, God had provided a means to salvation. The cherries were also a symbol of hope that came from an old Christian legend. According to the story, Mary and Joseph were walking in a garden full of cherries when Mary told him about the visitation of the angel. Joseph didn't believe her, and afterward, when she asked him to pick her some cherries, he refused. Miraculously the branches of the cherry trees bent so low that Mary could reach them.

For God so loved the world,
that he gave his only begotten Son,
that whosoever believeth in him
should not perish, but have everlasting life.

JOHN 3:16 KJV

He became the author of
eternal salvation unto all them
that obey him.

HEBREWS 5:9 KJV

Modern-Day Paradise Tree

Decorate your tree with apple and cherry decorations made of wood, resin, plastic, or any other material.

WHITE WAFERS
(not edible)

MATERIALS

white bake-clay
two ⅛-inch lattice strips
white satin ribbon for hanging

cross pendant
X-acto knife
white glue

Trace pattern outline onto sturdy cardboard and cut out. Roll slab of clay between ⅛-inch lattice strips. Use pattern to cut circle from clay; bore a hanging hole in ornament using a needle and following open circle on pattern for position. Emboss circle with a cross pendant by pressing the cross firmly into the clay. Bake according to clay instructions. Make a hanging loop with white satin ribbon and thread through hole.

The Christbaum

The oldest Christmas tree to be decorated and placed in the parlor is described in a 1605 travel diary by an unidentified visitor to Strasbourg. This traveler saw fir trees hung with paper roses of many different colors, as well as apples, flat wafers, gilded candies, and sugar. In early Christian art, the rose was a symbol for Mary, Jesus' mother, and the flat wafers were the communion symbol for Christ. A tree decorated with these wafers or cookies became known as a *Christbaum*.

The Christbaum Tree

These trees were decorated with roses, a tradition that was rooted in the legend that on the night of Christ's birth, flowers and trees miraculously blossomed the world over. This legend gave rise to the practice of decorating the Christmas tree with paper roses. Through the ages people added their own ideas to the Christbaum. Christ-bundles were hung from the tree—little packets filled with candy, sugarplums, and cakes—reflecting the joyous and generous spirit of Christmas when all gifts came from the Christ child.

In time, pastries began to replace communion wafers as decorations. They were made in two colors: White dough was shaped into flowers, bells, stars, angels, and hearts, while brown dough was used to make figures of men and animals.

Paper Rose Ornaments for a Modern-Day Christbaum

MATERIALS

tissue paper, red or white
florist's wire
green florist's tape

scissors
ruler
pencil

Cut one 3-inch and one 4-inch square of tissue paper. Crumple 3-inch square into a ball; place ball at one corner of 4-inch square. Fold opposite corner of 4-inch square toward ball, sandwiching ball between layers of tissue and forming a triangle. Next, fold other 2 corners of triangle toward ball, then roll and twist folded paper to resemble a tight bud, with crumpled ball at base of bud. Wrap floral wire around base of bud, securing paper. Trace pattern for rose petal 7 times onto tissue paper; cut out 7 petals. Add petals all around bud, one at a time, and with straight bottom edges even with base of bud; wrap with wire to secure. When last petal has been added, make a $1^3/_4$-inch stem with length of doubled wire. Wrap base of flower with florist's tape, covering wiring; continue down to cover stem. Pull tape taut while wrapping; wrap tightly for a firm, straight stem. Twist stem around tree branch.

"White Dough" Pretzels for Modern-Day Christbaum

MATERIALS

cardboard for pattern

white bake-clay

two ¼-inch lattice strips

satin ribbon for hanging

Trace entire pattern of a pretzel onto cardboard. Cut out, including inner sections. Roll slab of clay between ¼-inch lattice strips. Use pattern to cut pretzel shape from clay. Bake according to clay instructions. Thread satin ribbon through bottom hole of pretzel; tie for hanging loop.

Nativity Scene

To remind your children of the true center of Christmas (the baby Jesus) make a hanging nativity scene for the tree using a knobby gourd. Saw off the front of the gourd to make a window for crèche figures. Let your children model these figures from clay.

For the Antique Lover:
Unusual Tree Stands

- Place a small tree in an old shopping basket on wheels, or use an old apple basket or woven hamper.

- Use an old enamelware pot or breadbox as a colorful tree stand.

- Turn a rustic stool upside down and allow potted tree to rest between the legs.

- Use old pottery or crocks as a tree stand.

- Use a copper steamer as tree stand.

Pomander Candle Ornaments

Cut room for a tea candle in the top of an orange; use an embroidery needle to pierce a design into orange and press cloves into the holes. Hang the ornament using copper wire.

Spend a restful evening gazing at a small tree full of these lit ornaments, making sure someone is always present while you allow the candles to burn.

Antique Graduated Grain Measures

Stacked one on top of another, these make a nice, tiered, tabletop tree. Decorate the ledges that are formed with laurel leaves, nuts, votive candles, figurines, or any other miniatures of your choice. Top the smallest box with a tiny artificial evergreen to continue the "tree" theme.

*Let us now go even unto Bethlehem,
and see this thing which is come to pass,
which the Lord hath made known unto us.*

LUKE 2:15 KJV

Away in a manger,
no crib for a bed,
The little Lord Jesus laid down His sweet head;
The stars in the bright sky looked down where He lay,
The little Lord Jesus, asleep on the hay.

ANONYMOUS

Trees to Display Antique Collections

- A miniature tree could display an antique button collection. The buttons are easy to thread, and a nice variety of shapes, sizes, and colors would make a pretty tree.

- Antique silver spoons make beautiful decorations. They can be hung, handle down and bowl of spoon toward top, with silver thread tied below the bowl part. Little white lights reflecting off these spoons would be pretty.

- Decorate a small tree with heirloom lace, doilies, or hankies.

- Or decorate a tree with a miniature bottle collection.

Baby Shower Tree

If someone is expecting a baby around Christmas, decorate a tree for a baby shower with little baby necessities: brush and comb sets, safety pins, washcloths, pacifiers, teething rings, etc.

*And whoso shall receive
one such little child in my name receiveth me.*

MATTHEW 18:5 KJV

Wedding Shower Tree

How about a tree that could be decorated for a couple with a Christmas wedding? It could be covered with fanned money, gift certificates, or other small gifts, along with wedding announcements, printed reception napkins, etc.

The Lichstock

About the time evergreens were becoming popular as Christmas trees, a Christmas treelike decoration called a "pyramid" also came into use. Cut evergreen boughs were wrapped around open pyramid-shaped wooden frames, which were then decorated with candles and pastry. This candle-covered tree, called a *lichstock,* eventually developed into the candlelit Christmas tree, but for a long time the *lichstock* and *Christbaum* existed side by side.

Advent Tree

Decorate with key Bible verses that have been decoupaged on glass balls that are hung at intervals as the family reads the story of the birth of the Christ child.

And the Word was made flesh,
and dwelt among us,
(and we beheld his glory,
the glory as of the only begotten of the Father,)
full of grace and truth.

JOHN 1:14 KJV

Hark, the herald angels sing,
"Glory to the newborn King!"

SAMUEL WESLEY

Doll Clothes Tree

Surprise a little girl who loves Barbies or other small dolls with a small tree in her room hung with doll clothes, instead of, or in addition to, a Christmas stocking.

Baseball Card Tree

For a youngster who likes collecting baseball cards, hang a little tree with baseball cards that have been laminated or placed in sleeves.

Sugartrees

Trees in the eighteenth century were decorated with many kinds of sweet confections, as well as apples and fruits and nuts. They were often called "sugartrees." On the evening of Twelfth Night or Epiphany, January 6, which commemorates the arrival of the Magi at Bethlehem, the sugartrees were shaken and the sweets eaten.

Memory Tree

If your children have all grown up and moved away, how about decorating two trees: one fancy one and one Memory Tree that holds all the ornaments constructed by your children over the years?

Southwestern Tree

For those who live in the Southwest and are proud of their heritage, how about a tree decorated with chili peppers, cacti, minisaddles, boots, cowboy hats, burros, Indian teepees, and Indian drums? There are entire websites devoted to selling Southwestern Christmas decorations.

The Seamstress's Tree

Decorate your tree with small sewing items, such as thimbles, spools, and silver scissors.

Father Christmas Tree

There are many, many different Santa ornaments made from so many different materials and springing from so many different national heritages. To keep your perspective, remember to include my favorite—the old saint bowing beside the manger to the Christ child.

Lamb Tree

Cover a tree with different types of lambs, to remind you of the One whose birthday we celebrate.

Behold the Lamb of God,
which taketh away the sin of the world.

JOHN 1:29 KJV

Children's Theme Trees

Children enjoy trees with one theme. Here are some decoration possibilities:

animals	dolls
toys	dime-store gifts
fairy-tale characters	"jewels"
snowflakes	birds
bells	buttons and bows
stars	

English Christmas Trees

Queen Victoria's husband, Prince Albert, who came from the German province of Saxe-Coburg, is generally credited with introducing the Christmas tree to England after the birth of their first son in 1841. The origin of the story about Prince Albert's connection with Christmas trees may have been a full-page illustration in an 1848 edition of the *Illustrated London News* showing one of Albert's trees at Windsor. Because Victorians often imitated the royal family, the custom spread rapidly.

This motley collection of odd objects,
clustering on the tree like magic fruit
. . .made lively realisation of
the fancies of childhood;
and set me thinking
how all the trees that grow
and all the things that
come into existence on the earth,
have their wild adornments
at that well-remembered time.

CHARLES DICKENS

Care of the Tree

If the needles feel rubbery and alive, and if the cut end exudes a gummy, sticky substance, the tree will be reasonably fresh. Avoid trees whose needles have turned brown in spots or that fall when shaken gently. Trees with a trunk length from seven to ten inches below the lowest usable branch will need to be recut for placement.

Allow your tree to remain outdoors, protected from the sun until ready for use. Rain and snow are good for it, or you may spray the whole tree once or twice to keep the needles moist. Recut the trunk on a deep diagonal before placing in the stand to expose as much surface for water consumption as possible. Add either of the following to the water as a stimulant: 1 cup of sugar, molasses, or syrup, or 1 teaspoonful of plant fertilizer, to each quart of water.

Do not take the tree directly into your heated room from outside. Instead, take it first to a cool basement for a day, then move it to its final location. A gradual transition will be less of a shock and will help prolong its beauty and life.

Set the Mood

BLUE TREE LIGHTS:
make us think of a cold frosty night;

WHITE TREE LIGHTS: imply purity;

MULTICOLORED TREE LIGHTS: are gay and festive.

Create a Winter Scene

As an under-the-tree decoration, cover stacked books or magazines with a white sheet and cotton batting. Create scenes with skiers, skaters, churchgoers, wise men, shepherds, etc. Children will particularly enjoy arranging and rearranging the scene.

Primitive Trees

For trees with a primitive feeling, fireproofed straw makes a great undertree treatment and reminds us of Christ's humble birth. Emphasize the natural beauty of the tree by making ropes or garlands of acorns, walnuts, hazelnuts, peanuts, and almonds. Hang straw figures, and instead of stringing lights on this tree, emphasize the subtle coloring of the decorations using a green or yellow reflector flood lamp of 150 watts.

The Ceppo Tree

Francis of Assisi, attempting to make the story of Christ's birth more understandable to the people of the Italian countryside, was the first to use small carved figures to depict the characters. The idea appealed to the people, and they, in turn, carved similar figures to relate the story to their children. These early nativity scenes evolved into pyramid-shaped structures that contained several shelves on which the nativity figures were placed. Above them were small trinkets and figurines of animals, birds, and angels. The figures were collected or made with loving care and handed down from generation to generation.

Piñata Tree

Make small piñatas in the form of bells, stars, animals, and balls from fabric, felt, or foil paper. Cut 2 pieces of each design and sew, glue, or staple them together. Decorate with paper streamers, faces, and comical hats. Fill with fancy candies, nuts, miniature toys, and flowers.

Then fill 5-inch squares of colored cellophane with confetti. Draw up the corners of the cellophane squares and tie with a 9-inch length of ribbon. Allow the ends of the cellophane to extend above the ribbon to resemble flower petals.

Next shape #10 wire into a pyramid-shaped tree. Wire a length of 1-inch hemp rope to this form and paint it red. Suspend the tree from the ceiling by a rope fastened to the top, allowing enough rope to swing tree back and forth and to raise and lower it. Tie the gift piñatas and the confetti piñatas to the tips of the wire "branches." At midnight, tell each Christmas guest to grab 1 cellophane piñata from the tree, which you have set in motion. After the confetti piñatas are broken, each person in turn then tries to claim a gift piñata from the swinging tree.

The Dog's Tree

Children will enjoy creating a special tree for a favorite pet. Ask the butcher for extra bones and hang them on the tree with dog toys, biscuits, and other canine yummies.

Advent Tree

To make a tree decoration for your door, cut a tree form, trunk, and base from plywood and a similar shape from $1/2$-inch mesh hardware cloth. Tack the hardware cloth to the plywood. Rub the trunk with brown shoe polish. Cut 4-inch lengths of arborvitae and weave them into the mesh openings. Make sure your tree and base are well filled and present a rounded appearance. Hang miniature figures, animals, or toys on the tree. When children visit tell them to select and take home a figure. Of course, you will need to redecorate often, but the tree will be fun for all.

American Christmas Trees

Tree trimming was not widely practiced in the United States until after the Civil War. Here, as abroad, the first trees were small enough to be set on tables. Initially, Christmas trees were hung with edibles, but by 1860 city folk could purchase special toys and imported glass ornaments. Families living in rural areas exercised their ingenuity and contrived tree ornaments out of spare materials. Favorite decorations included candles, cookies, popcorn strings, gilded walnuts, candy-filled cornucopias, blown and colored eggs, paper chains and cutouts, baskets, small flags, simple toys, carvings, and little gifts.

Christmas Dinner Table Tree

Use round or oval mirror for the base. Cut 4-inch lengths of yew and wire them to a wrought iron candle tree with #25 wire. Start at the tips and work toward the center by placing three 4-inch lengths of yew on the frame. Bind with #32 wire. Place a second group of yew on the frame, making sure to overlap the stems of the previous placement. Continue in this manner until the tree is covered. Trim slightly if needed. Place red candles in the holders and stand the tree on the mirror. Tuck short lengths of greens under the mirror base. Add small nativity figures at the base.

The Yew Sleigh Tree

This tree can be made from several branches of yew assembled to resemble a tree. Place a pinpoint in the bottom of a miniature table-top sleigh. Wedge a good-sized potato on the pinpoint and insert the yew into the potato. The moisture in the potato will keep the greens fresh. Decorate the tree with red berries thrust into the greens and potato. Place gifts near the sleigh.

Designs from Plant Materials

The seedpods from many flowers such as iris, yucca, oriental poppy, goldenrod, rose hips, buckwheat blossoms, milkweed pods, sumac berries, and eucalyptus pods can be used as ornaments. They are lovely in their natural state or they can be gilded, silvered, or painted. Pinecones add interesting variety of design. Try cutting through the cone with a sharp knife or small saw to form rosettes that resemble flowers. The stem end is especially interesting. Paint, gild, silver, or use in their natural state. Wind wires around the segments so they cannot be seen and use to hang.

An American Tradition

In 1900, only one out of every five American families had a Christmas tree. Most children, however, probably enjoyed one at school or at a neighbor's house—and all children wished for a tree of their own. By 1910, in most parts of America, their dream had come true—nearly every family had a tree at home. And by 1930, the Christmas tree had become an American tradition.

Egg Shell Ornaments

Punch a pinhole in the top and the bottom of the shell. Blow gently through one end so that the contents are expelled. Wash the shell, and let dry thoroughly. Paint any color you like and decorate with sequins, beads, paper stripping, bits of felt, and paper. Funny heads can be made by painting in features or pasting on paper eyes, noses, and mouths. Glue perky paper hats to the top of the head.

Mirror Plaques for the Tree

Paint designs on pocket mirrors with poster paint. With glue, add beads, paper stripping, angel hair, bits of scouring pads, and cotton. With pinking shears cut a backing of felt 1 inch larger than the dimensions of the mirror. Place a strip of ribbon between the felt and the mirror. Glue the mirror to the felt.

Jesse Tree

This is a special tree that reminds children of the Old Testament stories that pointed to the coming of Christ. You may want to use a smaller Christmas tree for this, or even a large houseplant. Each ornament for the tree symbolizes an Old Testament story; for instance, a ladder represents Jacob; little tablets, the law of Moses; a rainbow, the story of Noah; a harp for David; a trumpet for the walls of Jericho; a sheaf of wheat for Ruth and Naomi; a scroll, Isaiah's prophecy; and so on. Use your knowledge of the Bible to come up with your own ornament ideas, and ask your children for their help. Each night of Advent, tell an Old Testament story and have a child hang on the Jesse Tree the ornament that goes with that story. This will help children understand the connection between Christ's coming and the Old Testament.

The Giving Tree

Have a small second Christmas tree in your house where throughout Advent children can place gifts for the needy. (Or you could do this activity at church for Sunday school classes or groups.) They might want to use their own spending money to buy gifts, or they can wrap new toys that they would like to share with someone who has less than they have. At the end of Advent, go together as a group to deliver the gifts to a local shelter or other charity.

Trimming the Tree

This activity takes the hassle out of decorating the tree. After you set up your Christmas tree, leave it bare except for the lights. Place the ornaments in a box beside the tree. Then each time a child does an act that expresses the true spirit of Christmas, he or she gets to hang a decoration on the tree. (Obviously, the decorations will need to be "child friendly.") Your tree may not end up looking like Martha Stewart decorated it. But it will be a testament to your children's love and goodwill for one another.

Their Very Own Trees

Young children often like to redecorate the tree every day. Here's an idea that avoids adult frustration and allows children to redecorate to their hearts' content. Cut small branches from shrubbery or use branches trimmed off of your Christmas tree. Place the branches in a large can filled with gravel. Then give the children an assortment of unbreakable decorations and place each child's "tree" in his or her bedroom. As they grow older, you can let them put lights on the branches as well. They'll spend a lot of time in their rooms simply watching their "trees."

Taking Down the Tree

The old-fashioned edible Christmas tree decorations gave children a pleasure to anticipate that has been lost today. In the past, all through the holidays the tantalizing cookies and candies that hung on the tree were forbidden fruit; they had to stay in place until the tree was taken down on Twelfth Night, when they could finally be eaten. Back then, taking down the tree was not the dismal, anticlimactic chore it is today; instead, it was the much awaited, delicious climax to the Christmas season.

Modern-day families may not want to encourage an orgy of sweets—but to make taking down the tree a little less painful, wrap a few small extra gifts and hide them among the tree's branches, to be opened after all the dismantling is complete. Wrap these after-Christmas presents in gold paper, as "gifts of gold" are part of the Epiphany tradition, in remembrance of the wise men's gifts to the Christ child.

Family Tree

MATERIALS

18-inch-long paper-covered wire
(for example, 36 pieces for
18 family members)
boxwood leaves
1½-inch photo of each family
member

glue
dried flowers
ribbon
6 x 6-inch piece of
1½-inch thick
green Styrofoam
sheet moss

Begin by twisting together all of the pieces of covered wire about 2 inches from the bottom and continue upwards about 6 inches. Fan the bottom pieces out to form the "roots" of the tree. At the top of the twist, begin to divide the "branches" into groups of 4, fanning them out on both sides of the tree. Separate the strands of each group of 4 and fan out also. Trim ends of branches with scissors when finished to achieve realistic tree shape. Glue a 2-inch ribbon loop to each photo. Then glue around perimeter of each photo and sprinkle with dried flowers to create frame effect. Cover Styrofoam with sheet moss and stick roots of tree in Styrofoam. Glue boxwood leaves to tree branches to simulate an evergreen tree and hang photos of family members to tree in generational order.

Alternative Christmas Tree

MATERIALS

glossy evergreen clippings,
   such as boxwood
rose hips
false berries
damp sphagnum moss
1-inch wire mesh netting

wire cutters
7-inch-diameter
   flowerpot
florist's adhesive tape
scissors
florist's scissors

Place the moss on the wire mesh netting and turn corners into center to enclose, crushing into a ball shape. Place ball in the flowerpot and secure with 2 or 3 pieces of adhesive tape. Cut evergreens to approximately equal lengths and push stems in the wire ball until completely filled in. Push in rose hips and false berries.

Advent for the Birds

At the beginning of December have the kids string popcorn and cranberries for a "bird's Christmas tree." They can also decorate the tree with pinecones covered with cheap peanut butter and then rolled in birdseed. This activity reminds children that God's love and care extend even to the natural world around us.

Surprise Rolls for the Tree

MATERIALS
cardboard tubing from wrapping paper, paper towels,
waxed paper, aluminum foil, or toilet tissue
brightly colored crepe paper
long piece of ribbon for curling
assorted candies, treats, and snacks

Cut tubes into equal-length sections (about 3½ inches long). Place the cardboard tube on paper and roll up, pinching paper together at one end and tying with a piece of curling ribbon. Fill tube with treats, pinch other end, and tie with more curling ribbon. Open twisted ends, and decorate with glue and glitter or Christmas stickers.

Kissing Ball Ornaments

(for tree or hanging in doorways)

MATERIALS
2 wooden embroidery hoops   ribbons, trim, or beads
glue gun   mistletoe
glue sticks

Crisscross wooden embroidery hoops, placing one inside the other, so they are perpendicular, and glue together. Decorate with ribbons, trim, or beads and place sprig of mistletoe in the center. Tie a ribbon at the top for hanging.

Gingerbread-Friends Garland

MATERIALS

clay gingerbread men
red and white icing

$\frac{1}{8}$-inch red ribbon
scissors

Using oven-bake clay, make a batch of gingerbread men. Punch holes in each hand with a drinking straw and bake. After the "cookies" have cooled, outline and decorate using icing. Link the men together by threading thin ribbon through holes in their hands. Knot ribbon and trim the ends.

Heart-Sachet Tree Ornaments

MATERIALS

fabric
pinking shears
thread

potpourri
ribbon

Cut 2 pieces of fabric (cut through 2 layers at once) with pinking shears in the shape of a heart. With wrong sides of fabric together, machine-stitch around heart close to pinked edge, spooning in a tablespoon of potpourri when half sewn. Finish sewing and attach a ribbon loop to hang from tree.

Metal Foil Ornaments

MATERIALS

metal foil, in brass, copper, and aluminum (available from craft stores)

ballpoint pen

metallic thread (for hanging)

Draw a shape onto stiff paper and cut it out to create a pattern. Put the pattern on a piece of metal foil that is slightly larger than the pattern, and draw around it using a soft pencil. Place the foil on a pile of magazines with the pattern on top in the same position; remove ink cartridge from a ballpoint pen and go over the outline with the empty pen to draw freehand within the outline to create details, remembering to press hard all the time. Use a pair of strong scissors to cut out the design and pierce a hole at the top. Tie a loop of metallic thread through for hanging. Flatten foil gently with rolling pin if it has curled. The right side is the opposite side to the one worked on, which gives the metal a raised, "embossed" effect.

A Great Invention

Christmas tree hooks were one of the greatest inventions in Christmas tree history. They were first advertised in a wholesaler's catalogue in 1892:

> *It is a well-known fact, that heretofore it has taken the best part of Christmas Eve to trim a tree by tying strings or threads to the trinkets, and then tying these to the tree, thus taking about 2–3 hours of one person's time and labor to trim a tree with 100 articles. With these hooks, the same number can be applied in less than half an hour.*

Lace-Embossed Clay Tree Ornaments

MATERIALS

modeling compound clay

luncheon-sized plate

masking tape

piece of old lace or paper doilies

talcum powder

1x8-inch dowel rod

small straw

gold or silver thread

On a protected surface, tape luncheon plate facedown and lightly dust with talcum powder. Roll a 1-inch ball of modeling clay to an even thickness in the center of the plate using the dowel rod. Place lace or doily over the clay and roll again to emboss pattern into the clay. Remove lace and push straw through top of the ornament to form a hole through which metallic thread may be strung to hang ornament. These ornaments may also be painted.

Nature's Ornaments

- Place orange rings cut in $\frac{1}{4}$-inch slices on an oven rack at lowest temperature and dry for 1 hour. Just below the peel, push a hole through with knife tip and thread with a ribbon and tie to tree.

- Bundle together 3 or 4 cinnamon sticks with a pretty ribbon and glue cranberries to the ribbon with a glue gun; place bundle on tree branches.

- Thread tiny kumquats onto medium stub wires and loop circlets over tree branches or tie with contrasting ribbons.

- Tie ribbon or yarn around top petals of a pinecone for hanging, and glue beads on cone as ornaments.

Matzebaum

In the nineteenth century, the Pennsylvania Germans decorated their trees with *matzebaum,* wafer-thin, 2x4-inch cakes made from almond paste, sugar, and egg whites. Before being baked, each cake was pressed with a carved wooden mold that left raised images of animals, birds, or flowers on the face of the cookie. After baking, matzebaum were usually painted with homemade vegetable dyes. Most of the cookies were eaten by the children when the Christmas tree was dismantled, but a few were laid away and brought out to decorate the family tree year after year.

Thicker objects—vegetables, fruits, and animals—were also shaped from the same type of almond-flavored dough and called marzipan or marchpane. Marzipan originated in Persia and had been made in Germany since the Middle Ages. It was originally a delicacy consumed at court banquets and became a common Christmas confection during the eighteenth century.

Marzipan Potatoes

Materials

MARZIPAN:

1 lb pure almond paste
1½ c sifted confectioners' sugar

3 tbsp light corn syrup
¾ tsp vanilla

ALSO:

cinnamon
toothpick

needle
gold thread for hanging

Mix marzipan ingredients together and knead until smooth. Break off pieces of marzipan and roll into 1-inch-diameter shapes resembling potatoes; do not make balls perfectly round. When satisfied with shape, roll in cinnamon. Insert toothpick through one end of each potato for hanging hole. Allow potatoes to harden, then thread needle with 7-inch length of gold thread. Run needle and thread through hanging hole; knot ends.

Edible Decorations

*A*nother cookie hung on the Christmas tree was the white *springerle,* made of an egg dough seasoned with anise seeds. The smooth dough produced an excellent cameolike image when molded, and the cookies were often painted and then hung from the tree with a piece of string or a ribbon. Most of the molds were the work of professional German woodcarvers, and few families possessed these fancy cookie molds. Most households, though, had cookie cutters made by itinerant tinsmiths.

Springerles

Ingredients

3¼ c flour
¼ tsp baking powder
4 large eggs
1⅔ c sugar

1 tsp finely grated lemon zest
1 tsp anise extract
optional: 2–3 tbsp whole
or crushed anise seeds

Roll out the dough ¼-inch thick, using extra flour to keep the dough from sticking. Press molds firmly into dough, and then cut cookies apart with a knife. Sprinkle with anise seeds if desired. Use a spatula to transfer cookies to a greased baking sheet, ½ inch apart. (If cookies are to be used as a decoration, use a straw to take out a circle of dough where a loop can be inserted for hanging.) Set the cookies aside for 10–12 hours, and then bake at 300° F for 18–25 minutes, until the cookies are almost firm but not colored. If desired, decorate the cookies with a paintbrush and a wash made out of diluted food coloring. Insert yarn or ribbon loops and hang on the tree. Springerles are meant to be very hard, and they keep indefinitely. They will still be edible at the end of the Christmas season when you take down the tree.

Sugar Ring Cookies to Hang on the Tree

MATERIALS

dough (see recipe following)
compass
paper for pattern

darning needle
red or green yarn or ribbons
   for hanging

Preheat oven to 350° F. On paper draw 2 concentric circles ¾ inch and 2¼ inches in diameter. Cut around outer circle, then inner, leaving ring pattern. Roll out ball of dough to ⅛-inch thickness. Place ring pattern on dough and trace around edges with knife or darning needle; remove pattern. Repeat until all dough is used. Place cookies on sheets; leave plain or coat with colored sprinkles, tapping sprinkles lightly into the dough with the tip of your finger. Bake for 8–10 minutes or until golden brown. Cool on rack. For each cookie, cut 7-inch length of yarn or ribbon; thread through center of ring and knot ends.

DOUGH RECIPE

½ c softened butter or margarine
½ c sugar
2 eggs
½ tsp vanilla

1½ c flour
¾ tsp double-acting baking
   powder
¼ tsp salt

Combined softened butter or margarine and sugar and beat until creamy. Add eggs and vanilla, beating well. Add flour, baking powder, and salt; beat until well mixed. Form into ball and chill for 3 hours.

Cookie Decorations

Most of the cookies on nineteenth-century Christmas trees—spice, butter, and gingerbread—were thicker than today's cookies, often half an inch thick. Cookie-baking binges lasted for two solid weeks early in December. A "washbasketful" was a standard measure of cookies in Pennsylvania-Dutch kitchens. The housewife who didn't have at least several washbaskets full of cookies just wasn't ready for Christmas. And many of these went on the tree.

By the 1880s, in addition to gingerbread animals and people, flat gingerbread cakes were hung on the trees. They were decorated with colorful pictures pasted on with egg white.

Icing

(for cookie decorations)

2 egg whites   1¼ c confectioners' sugar
³⁄₈ tsp cream of tartar

Beat egg whites with whisk or electric beater until frothy and slightly thickened. Add cream of tartar and continue beating until whites hold a peak. Sift confectioners' sugar into whites, about ½ cup at a time, beating thoroughly between additions. Beat 5–8 minutes until icing is thick and smooth.

Cookies with Paper Cutouts to Hang on the Tree

MATERIALS

Dough and Icing
(see recipes on pages 360–361)
ruler
paper for pattern
knife
darning needle

prints of angels or other
motifs from
Christmas cards
curved cuticle scissors
paintbrush for icing
gold ribbon

Preheat oven to 325° F. On paper, draw a rectangle 3¼x4 inches; round the corners. Cut out pattern. Roll out dough between sheets of wax paper to ½-inch thickness. Place pattern on dough and trace around edges with knife or darning needle; remove pattern. Punch small hanging hole near center top of one short edge. Repeat until all dough is used. Place cookies on sheets. Bake for 35 minutes or until cookies are firm and brown. Cool completely. While cookies are baking and cooling, carefully cut out prints using curved cuticle scissors. When cookies are cool, cover the back of the print with a thin layer of icing. Press the iced side of the print on the center of the cookie. Thread hanging hole with gold ribbon; knot ends.

Gingerbread Dough

(for cookie decorations)

6 c flour
4 tsp ground ginger
1½ tsp ground cinnamon
1 tsp ground cloves
¼ tsp each: ground nutmeg,
    cardamom, salt

2 sticks butter or
    margarine
1 c firmly packed light
    brown sugar
½ c dark corn syrup
½ c light molasses

Sift flour and spices together in bowl. Combine butter, brown sugar, corn syrup, and molasses in saucepan and place over low heat until butter is melted and all ingredients are blended. Remove from heat. Combine 2 cups flour mixture and the butter mixture in mixing bowl and blend well. Continue adding remaining flour mixture, blending until dough is firm but pliable. Flour hands and knead dough until smooth and slightly sticky. If dough is too moist, add flour by the tablespoon. Refrigerate for 1 hour.

Stuffed Animal Ornaments

MATERIALS

animal cookie cutters or pattern
pencil
fabric—cotton, calico, felt, wool,
    suede cloth, leather
straight pins
scissors or pinking shears

sewing needle
colored thread
fiberfill, cotton batting, or
    shredded nylon
    stockings
colored yarn, buttons, or any
    other trim desired

Make a pattern by tracing a cookie cutter directly onto the fabric; trace a cardboard pattern, or draw a figure of your own, such as simple elephants, sheep, horses, chickens, and ducks. Pin the pattern onto a double layer of fabric. If the material will be sewn on the wrong side and turned right side out, add an additional ¼ inch to the pattern. With scissors or pinking shears, cut out the 2 layers of fabric along these lines. Sew the right sides together ¼ inch from the edge. Leave a 1-inch space open to insert the stuffing. Trim seam edges, turn right side out, and stuff with fiberfill, stockings, or other lightweight filler. Stitch up the stuffing hole. Add eyes (buttons may be used), tail, swings, or mane using scraps of fabric or yarn. Sew on a thread loop for hanging the ornament.

*C*hristmas tree decorations do not need
to be expensive. Our ancestors made most
of their decorations from things they found
in the natural world around them. The next
few pages contain instructions for ornaments that
you, too, can make from items you find
in nature (or purchase from
craft stores if the outdoor world
isn't handy for you).

Starfish Decorations

MATERIALS

dried starfish (can be purchased at most craft stores or at a beach store)

scissors
lightweight clear plastic fishing line

Wrap thin lightweight fishing line around the starfish as a hanger. Tie securely and hang.

Sand Dollar Decorations

MATERIALS

sand dollars (collected from the beach or purchased from craft or beach store)

red or green satin ribbon, $\frac{1}{4}$ inch wide
Christmas tree hanger

If you collect sand dollars on the beach, dry them thoroughly and then soak them in a strong bleach solution (3 parts bleach to 1 part water) for a day or until they are white. Rinse thoroughly with water and dry in the sun. Sand dollars are extremely fragile and must be handled with great care. When completely dry, tie a satin bow through the center hole in the sand dollar. Attach a tree hanger to the bow.

Pinecone Angel

MATERIALS

heavy scissors or flower clippers
3-inch pinecone
2 dried milkweed pods
    (gather them in the fall)
white glue
black felt pen with a fine point

hickory nut, small
    walnut, or other nut
    about ¼-inch high
small piece of string or
    yarn for hanger

Cut off the top bracts (petals) from the pinecone to make room for the angel's head, which is the nut. Take the milkweed pods, hollow side facing out, and push into the back of the cone to form wings. Glue and let dry. Make facial features on the nut head with the black felt pen, then glue it onto the cone. When dry, glue on a hanger of string or yarn.

Cornhusk Flower Decoration

MATERIALS

field corn with shucks attached
boiling water in a pan or kettle

knife or cleaver
scissors

Gather field corn in the fall after the first frost has turned the ears of corn down. Be careful to leave 2–3 inches of stem. Pull back the husks, exposing the entire ear. Using a knife or cleaver, cut away all but the last ½ inch of the ear, leaving approximately 3 rows of kernels, which will be used for the center of the flower. Return the husks to their original position, and cut each of them with the scissors to resemble petals. Carefully work over a kettle of boiling water and shape each petal with your hands. The steam makes the petals very pliable. The longer the husks are, the larger the flowers will be.

Popcorn and Red Pepper String

MATERIALS

sturdy white thread
long sewing needle
dried red peppers, 1 to 2
    inches long

freshly popped white popcorn,
    unsalted and unbuttered
    (One large bowl makes a
    makes a 5-foot chain.)

Thread the needle and put it through 1 red pepper either lengthwise or widthwise. Tie the thread securely around the pepper to form a knot. Thread the popcorn onto the string alternating peppers and popcorn. You can use 1 pepper to every 6 to 12 pieces of popcorn or alternate popcorn and peppers. Make the chain as long as you like. However, if it is over 6 feet long, the chain becomes difficult to handle. Several chains can be tied together before putting them on the tree. Only freshly popped corn should be used, because stale popcorn tends to shatter.

Corn Shuck Pig Decoration

MATERIALS

3-inch-long ear of corn, such as a small ear of popcorn, with the husks still attached
knife
water
straight pin
white glue
thread

Carefully remove the corncob, but leave the husks attached to the base. Trim off all but 2½ inches from the pointed end of the corncob and remove the kernels of corn. Dampen the husks. Slip the cob inside the husks, pointed end first. Pull the ends of the husks together and twist or braid them. Curl to form a tail. Secure with a pin until dry enough to glue together. Trim the base end of the corn shuck to form a snout. Cut a cornstalk in 4 equal lengths for legs. Be sure they are in proportion to the body. Glue them to the dry body. Cut a shorter cornstalk and split it to make 2 ears. Glue in place. Note: You may need to tie a bit of thread around the nose if the husks come loose from the base.

Black Walnut Owl Ornament

MATERIALS

2 medium-sized black walnut shells
small wire brush
pliers or bench vise
small hand or electric saw
straight pin
medium-grade sandpaper or file

household cement
tiny eye screw
metal or yarn hanger
optional—hand or
    electric drill

Select medium-sized black walnut shells. You will need ½ shell for the head and a whole walnut for the body. Note: Regular walnuts cannot be used. Clean the shells with a wire brush. Cut 1 shell into 2 equal parts following the seam line as closely as possible. To cut, place the shell in a bench vise and saw with either a handsaw or an electric saw. Or hold the shell with pliers and feed it into the saw blade very slowly. (Don't try to hold the shell in your hand; you may cut your finger.)

Clean out the meat from the split walnut with a straight pin. Sand the cut side of this shell to eliminate saw marks. Sand the top of the whole shell and the bottom of the half shell to obtain the smooth surface needed for gluing together. The bottom of the body can also be sanded smooth to allow the owl to stand alone. Using a vise to hold the head, drill a small hole for an eye screw at the top of head. Glue the head to the body with household cement and let it set for about 10 hours. Add a metal or yarn hanger. You can drill small holes in the back of the head through the eye holes to allow light to shine through.

Shell Wreath

(to hang on the tree or door)

MATERIALS

X-acto knife or sturdy scissors
corrugated cardboard (4 inches x
   4 inches x ¼-inch thick—
   2 thin pieces can be glued
   together)

household cement
red velvet ribbon, ¼-inch
   wide and 24 inches long
shells in assorted sizes

With the X-acto knife or the scissors, cut the cardboard into a circle 4 inches in diameter, then cut a circle 2 inches in diameter out of the center. Glue a piece of the velvet ribbon around the outside edge of the circle. Glue the rest of the ribbon through the center and tie it into a bow for a hanger.

Using shells picked up at the beach, or purchased, start at the top of the circle and glue on 1 of the larger shells. Glue other larger shells around the edges at well-spaced intervals. Then put in shells of all kinds, textures, sizes, and colors to form a pleasing pattern. Use pieces of spiral cord and tiny shells to fill in any gaps. No 2 wreaths will be alike.

Hemlock String

MATERIALS

long, sharp needle   dried hemlock cones
lightweight clear plastic fishing line

Thread the needle and push it through 1 hemlock cone. Tie the fishing line firmly around the first cone to secure it. Thread the rest of the cones onto the fishing line and secure the last cone as you did the first. String the cones through the middle or end to end. Make the chain as long as you wish.

Acorn Box Ornament

Remove the cap from a newly fallen acorn. Carve out the white circle underneath and remove the soft meat from inside the acorn. Wrap fine-grade sandpaper around a pencil eraser and smooth the inside of the acorn shell. Stain the outside with wood stain and allow to dry overnight. Select a cork that fits snugly into the acorn cap. Shorten the cork and carve to fit into the acorn opening. Smooth the cork with sandpaper and glue into cap. Drill a hole through the acorn's stem, and attach a loop of ribbon.

Topiaries

Topiaries are a variety of tabletop Christmas tree. The custom of training plants to grow in topiary form originated with the Romans and was more recently popular with the Victorians, who created topiaries from wire and filled them with moss, greenery, and flowers. Place topiaries where they can be enjoyed close-up—on sideboards, mantels, or tabletops. Fill them with oranges, lady apples, limes, and pomegranates. For greenery, use whatever you find in your backyard: pine, spruce, ivy, or holly. Use an interesting vase, garden accessory, or pottery bowl as a pedestal.

Lemon Topiary

MATERIALS

length of chicken wire
small, white-painted pinecones
available at craft stores or
floral shops

craft foam cone
bundle of florist's picks
fresh lemons
laurel leaves

Wrap the length of chicken wire around the cone from top to bottom to support the weight of the lemons. Nestle the wire-covered cone in a sturdy container, such as a moss-blanketed terra-cotta pot. Arrange the lemons on the cone in circular rows, working from the base to the tip and pressing the lemons into the foam with the florist's picks. In the same way, fill in the tree with pinecones, randomly spacing them along the lemons. For a green flourish, tuck in fresh laurel sprigs, allowing them to fan over the lemons and the pinecones.

A Kitchen Tree

Since so many holiday activities take place in the kitchen, this room deserves its own special tree. Place a little evergreen in a safe little nook of your kitchen and decorate it with dainty lady apples. Just slightly larger than sugarplums, they create a simple and beautiful tree and can be hung from golden metallic ribbon hangers secured to the apples with straight pins.

Rosemary Trees

Another decoration for the kitchen, the Rosemary Tree is both useful and lovely. Training these little trees takes some time and patience, though. Plant a straight-rooted cutting of rosemary in a pot of sterile, prepackaged soil. Place a stake in the soil by the plant. Loosely secure the plant to the stake with twist ties or raffia. When the plant reaches the desired height, clip the branches of a medium-sized plant into the familiar Christmas tree shape. To maintain, keep in sunlight, turning every few days for even growth. Keep plants moist but be sure not to overwater.

Sandpaper Man and Reindeer

MATERIALS

coarse sandpaper
pencil
strong scissors
white glue
felt scraps—red, green, blue,
    white, and black

scraps of green
    medium-sized rickrack
yarn
cotton

Trace the outlines of the man and reindeer on the smooth sides of 2 pieces of sandpaper. Cut out both shapes and glue the smooth sides together. Let dry. Decorate as follows: Use felt for eyes, mouth, hat, trousers, and belt, rickrack for suspenders, yarn in strips for bangs under the hat, and cotton for a beard. Decorate both sides. Make a yarn loop at the top of the hat for a hanger. Give the reindeer a cotton tail, a harness made out of rickrack or yarn, an eye of black felt, and a red felt nose.

Clustered Glass Balls

Recycle small, faded glass Christmas balls by stringing three or four different colors together on a strand of wire and add a few decorative leaves.

Paper Silhouettes Garland

MATERIALS

colored construction paper   scissors
pencil

Decide which figure you want to make. You can make a string of animals, such as bears or elephants, or a set of figures, such as angels or snowmen. Fold the construction paper into several layers wide enough to accommodate the figure you have chosen and thick enough to make the chain the length you desire. On the folded construction paper, trace the pattern given or draw around your favorite cookie cutter. Cut out the figure, being careful to leave part of the folded area on each side of the shape intact. If the folds are cut through entirely, the figures will not form a chain and will instead be separate and unattached to one another. After the cutting is completed, open the paper figures and find a chain to surround the tree!

Fruitful Trees

Using contrasting colors of sheer organdy, wrap dried oranges, other lightweight commercially freeze-dried fruit, or millinery fruit (cherries, blueberries, pears, apples, grapes, etc.) with two 12-inch-long pieces and tie together with a satin ribbon to hang from the tree.

Feather Trees

This Christmas decoration was created by the Germans, who loved to celebrate the holiday in a variety of delightful ways. Heavy wire branches were wrapped with feathers, usually from turkeys or geese, and sometimes swans. The feathers were dyed a dark green, giving the branches a natural look.

The first feather trees probably arrived in this country with German immigrants. Most measured from $2^1/_2$–3 feet in height with collapsible wire branches and would have been easily transported in steamer trunks. By the turn of the century, American department stores and mail-order catalogs were offering feather trees for sale. The passage of time brought variations to the details of the feather trees. They became available with different colored or shaped bases, as well as different colors for the feathers and berries. By the end of World War II, trees with built-in electric lights became available. By the 1950s, however, most stores and catalogs no longer sold feather trees, since the development of cellophane, as well as Visca, a dark green strawlike rayon, entered the artificial tree marketplace. But because of the soaring interest in American folk art and vintage holiday decorations, rare vintage feather trees are highly valued, fetching as much as one hundred dollars per foot or more!

Tree Farming

In 1909, the Forest Service estimated that five million Christmas trees were cut, and Christmas tree critics became more vocal every year until by the 1920s conservationists had a well-organized campaign. The Christmas tree trade had been buying the rights to evergreens along the roadsides and then felling every tree in sight, but now they finally realized that they were bringing a lot of criticism on themselves by cutting only the trees that were the easiest to get to market. The cutters began to thin rather than to level the trees along the highways, and sound conservation practices became more prevalent.

Christmas tree cultivation became a profitable business in many parts of the country. Farmers found it a good way to use rocky upland pastures and pieces of land not suited to other farming. In the 1930s, Franklin D. Roosevelt was the country's best-known Christmas tree farmer. He helped popularize the concept by growing Christmas trees on his estate at Hyde Park, New York.

Musical Tree

Hang the branches with miniature instruments, musical scales, and treble and G clefs.

Queen Anne's Lace Tree

Use dried Queen Anne's lace blossoms to decorate a Christmas tree. The blossoms can be picked in various stages of development for variety. Lovely in their natural state, the dried flowers can also be sprayed with white, gold, or silver paint.

Electric Christmas

The frustrating and dangerous problem of the Christmas tree candle was that it would not stand perfectly upright, no matter how carefully the tree trimmer tried to place it on a bough. In 1882, just three years after the invention of the electric lightbulb, the world's first electrically lighted Christmas tree was decorated in New York City at the home of Edward Johnson, a colleague of Thomas Edison.

Spruce Saplings

These young trees make thoughtful, environment-friendly gifts to give to holiday guests. Place a waterproof saucer on a large unfinished square of burlap. Set a tree, still in its nursery pot, onto the saucer. Gather the burlap around the pot and tie it in place with a festive ribbon bow. Then top with gilded stars. Assemble the saplings on your buffet to create your own little grove of trees.

Mossy Tabletop Trees

MATERIALS

plaster of paris
large stick for use as the trunk
terra-cotta pot
craft foam cone
florist's tape

spray adhesive
sheet moss
plastic bucket to be
    concealed in the
    pot

Mix the plaster of paris according to the package directions. Quickly pour the plaster mixture into the plastic bucket. Before the plaster hardens, insert the stick trunk into the center of the bucket; hold the trunk upright with a brace of florist's tape until the plaster completely hardens. Coat the top of the cone with spray adhesive. Press small, easy-to-manage pieces of sheet moss onto the adhesive-coated area. Once the top is covered, spray the adhesive on the bottom of the cone and wrap the remaining area with moss. Assemble the tree by pressing the bottom of the cone onto the top of the trunk. Conceal the plaster with sheet moss. Place the tree in the terra-cotta pot. Decorate the tree as desired using a strand of wooden beads, securing the thread at intervals with straight pins, or use dried vine or French wired ribbon. Add miniature ornaments to continue the diminutive scale.

Noah's Ark Tree

Decorate tree with animal figures and tiny arks.

Christmas Fragrance

Hang homemade potpourri sachets from your tree to enhance the evergreen fragrance of your Christmas tree. Mix:

1 c lavender flowers	2 tbsp each ground
8 c dried rose petals	allspice, ground
1 tbsp ground cloves	cinnamon, and
4 drops rose oil	ground orrisroot

Seal in an airtight container for six weeks before wrapping in pieces of meshed material secured with satin ribbons.

Grape Ornaments

Make bunches of grapes using tiny glass ornaments. Assemble about 25 glass balls of the same color, ranging in size from ⅝ inch to 1 inch. Remove the wire hanger from one ⅝-inch ball. Fold the tip of a pipe cleaner into a hook and poke it into the opening, so that it catches inside the ball and holds it securely. String the remaining balls on the pipe cleaner by their wire hangers, increasing the size as you go. Make a tendril by coiling another piece of pipe cleaner around a nail. Twist the tendril, together with a fabric leaf, to pipe-cleaner stem to finish the cluster.

Christmas Tree Prayer

This year, Lord, may our Christmas tree remind us
that our life in You will never die.
As we gather 'round its lights and bright decorations,
remind us to speak only words of love,
in honor of You, the Prince of Love,
whose birth we celebrate.

Amen.